AN INESCAPABLE FATE

a Josh and Abby novel - Book 3

by

Courtney Spencer

Print ISBN 978-1-7388087-3-1

Keep reading after the novel for a preview of something new by Courtney Spencer:

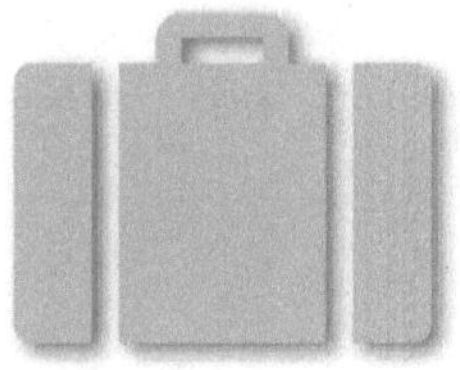

OTHER TITLES BY Courtney Spencer:

An Impossible Circumstance: a Josh & Abby novel – Book 1 *(2023)*

**Digital download available on Amazon Kindle and Apple Books. Paperback available on Amazon.*

An Irrepressible Desire: a Josh & Abby novel – Book 2 *(2024)*

**Digital download available on Amazon Kindle and Apple Books. Paperback available on Amazon.*

The What if Widow *(2023)*

**Digital download available on Amazon Kindle and Apple Books. Paperback available on Amazon.*

Follow **@courtneyspencerauthor** for the latest news on upcoming projects

Accompanying Playlist

If You Ever Want To Be in Love – James Bay

Habits - Gary Clark Jr.

Before You Go - Lewis Capaldi

Guilty as Sin? - Taylor Swift

Work Song - Hozier

Beautiful Things - Benson Boone

Northern Attitude - Noah Khan & Hozier

The Door - Teddy Swims

Taste - Sabrina Carpenter

She Will Be Loved - Maroon 5

The Other Man - Sloan

That's So True - Gracie Abrams

Cope - AKA Lisa

Safe and Sound (Taylor's Version) - Taylor Swift, Joy Williams & John Paul White

Birds of a Feather - Billie Eilish

Messy - Lola Young

Real Love Baby - Father John Misty

I Like Me Better - Lauv

Daisies - Justin Bieber

5 Days in May - Blue Rodeo

We Surrender - the East Pointers

Anything - Griff

How Bad Do U Want Me - Lady Gaga

From - Bon Iver

for those who were curious enough to see this through!

Josh and Abby

CONTENTS

Epigraph

Guilty as Sin?

"What if I roll the Stone away?
They're gonna crucify me anyway.
What if the way you hold me
is actually what's holy?
If long-suffering propriety
is what they want from me,
they don't know how
you've haunted me
so stunningly.
I choose you and me
... religiously."

—Taylor Swift, *The Tortured Poet's Department*

Prologue

A SECRET MEETING

April 25th, 2025 – Halifax, NS

Alexander Bouchard believed history was something learned—until he found himself living inside it.

The auditorium was supposed to be empty.

Alex glanced toward the doors for the third time, the EXIT sign glowing faintly in the darkness. The lights were off, but the space still felt too open, too exposed. He'd never been good at pretending things didn't affect him. Not the way Jane was.

"I think I heard someone come in here, Jane. You gotta stop," he urged through thick, uneven breaths.

She didn't look up at him. "I don't hear anything. Relax."

He shifted anyway, unease prickling along his spine. Alex had learned early on that quiet didn't always mean safe. Still, he let himself be pulled back into the moment, into her confidence, her certainty that the world bent easily around her.

A moment later, he reached for his pants and lightly nudged her shoulders, insisting, "I'm serious."

"Ugh," she scoffed. "You've got to be the only boy I know who has the audacity to stop me."

Then they both heard it.

A sharp clang. Something skittering across the auditorium's hardwood floor.

"See, I told you," he murmured into her ear as she stood.

They moved quickly then, retreating to the side of the stage, backs pressed against the wall as footsteps passed somewhere between the aisles.

Jane tilted her head toward him, eyes bright with irritation rather than fear. "I could have finished," she whispered.

"You're crazy," he said, glancing down into the intense brown eyes that challenged him at every turn.

She grinned, unapologetic. "How many girls do you know who'd skip Sociology to hook up with you?"

He smiled, recalling all the times in the last month that they had been meeting like this. "It really is a sociological experiment if you think about it. Why don't you just explain to Mr. Harris what you've been up to? I'm sure he'd give you bonus marks for dedication."

"Shut up, Alex," she snapped. "As if I'd tell anyone that we're… whatever."

He jolted back theatrically. "I know I agreed to this arrangement, but it still stings when you put it like that."

"Yeah, right. I'm not exactly your type either. Don't act like such a martyr."

He shrugged. "I don't care who knows."

It wasn't entirely true. Not because he wanted anything different, but because secrecy always changed things. Made them heavier. Made them matter more than they were supposed to.

His friends probably wouldn't even believe him if he told them he'd been secretly seeing the school's head cheerleader since March Break.

"Liar," she said.

"Fine, let's date for real. Let's tell people," he dared.

"No, you idiot," she hissed. "There are two months of school left. Let's see how things go and figure it out over the summer. Like we talked about."

"Whatever you say," he whispered. "We've got to get out of here."

"Can't risk Mr. Goody Two-shoes getting caught and losing his scholarship," she teased. "Tell me, how exactly is it that you're always free for our little excursions? Don't you have to go to class to be a nerd?"

Alex had always been careful about school and about his future. Early acceptance to Dalhousie had bought him a strange kind of freedom this semester, but it hadn't erased the quiet pressure he carried.

He knew what it was like to lose things. To watch families fracture. To grow up surrounded by stories no one wanted to finish telling.

"I'm not a nerd," he said. "I just get all my assignments done on time."

"Must be nice," she muttered. "I probably should have used you for studying instead."

He lowered his head to plant a gentle kiss on her stubborn mouth, catching her off guard.

Her breath deepened as she sank into him. Gestures like this always drew her back.

"Where's the fun in that?" he whispered.

Another beat of silence settled between them. The door echoed shut in the distance.

"I should go," Jane said, already stepping away. "I'll message you later."

Alex nodded. He watched Jane Barrington walk away without looking back, the sound of her footsteps fading into the building's hum.

Only later would he understand that nothing about this had ever been simple or contained.

That some stories didn't stay where you put them.

And that this one had already begun long before either of them knew how to name it.

PART 1: OLD FLAMES

Chapter 1: A LONG TIME

April 25th, 2025 – Halifax, NS

Abby burst through her front door, arms overloaded with binders and fabric swatches that slapped against her side as she moved. She kicked off her shoes and barrelled down the hall, dumping her day on the dining room table in a clatter as it smacked the wooden surface. A glance at the stove clock told her it was nearly six.

"A.J.," she shouted down the hall, "are you home?"

Her teenage son emerged from his main-floor bedroom. He made easy strides toward Abby, his hands tucked into his jeans, wavy pieces of his chestnut hair dangling over his forehead. A.J. was neither reserved nor shy, despite what his shadowed features might suggest. He carried his lanky six-foot frame with a confidence he definitely didn't inherit from his mother. Abby couldn't help but be reminded of her ex-husband, Christopher Bouchard, every time their son acted with authority he hadn't yet earned.

"Hey, Mom. How was your day?"

"Hi, bub. It was good." Abby was already sorting through the piles on the table. "What are you up to? Have you eaten?"

"No, not yet. I thought we were going out for dinner."

She glanced up. "We are?"

"Yeah," he said, moving in closer to peer over her shoulder. "You said you'd pay me in food if I escorted you to Costco tonight. It's time for a big order. All the heavy stuff."

"Oh shit," she said, remembering. "I did say that, didn't I?"

"Don't act so excited to spend time with me, Mother."

"Says the boy who had to be bribed to come with me in the first place," she said, teasing.

He shrugged, smiling. "Fair enough."

"Well, we might as well get going now. I've got tons of work to do this weekend."

"Alright," he said. "I'll grab my shoes."

* * *

She strolled the aisles, wishing she had the discipline to only reach for what she needed, but she couldn't resist the urge to browse. Costco FOMO—one of adulthood's more ridiculous afflictions. She'd hate to hear later from a friend that they'd scored a bargain she missed.

A.J. had wandered off. Or maybe she'd left him behind. He'd find her every few minutes and haphazardly throw something into the cart before taking off again.

Abby paused to consider a two-pack of parchment paper on sale. She still had some at home, but an extra 400 feet wouldn't go to waste. She continued down the aisle and spotted A.J. only a few metres ahead, chatting with an attractive young woman.

She coughed lightly to make her son aware of her approach and looked quickly at the girl, flashing her a timid smile.

"I've got to find my parents," the young woman said to A.J.

"Yeah, looks like my mom found me," he said, turning toward Abby.

"Here comes my dad, actually," Jane announced, peering over Abby's head to the end of the aisle. "Talk to you later, Alex."

Abby walked ahead while A.J. lingered, watching Jane make quick steps toward a tall, dark-haired man who looked relieved to spot her inside the busy store. Jane's dad carried two large bags of specialty coffee in one arm, extending his other to pat Jane on the shoulder.

"Have you seen your mother?" he asked. "I lost her in the seasonal section. It's a zoo in here."

"No," Jane answered. "I'll text her."

Jane smiled faintly at A.J. before turning to help her dad. As they carried on together, the man glanced down at A.J. with a curious look —part warning, part amusement. Along with the intensity of his eyes, a faint smile crept beneath the thick black stubble on his face. A.J. dipped his head politely and shuffled off to catch up with Abby.

"Did I hear that nice girl call you Alex?" Abby asked under her breath. "No one's called you that in ages."

"Um, yeah," he answered coolly. "It's like…an inside joke."

"Why would your name be a joke?" she pressed, teasing him.

"Don't worry about it, Mom."

Abby scrunched her nose playfully, signalling she'd drop it for now. While she was trying to navigate her way back into the main aisle of the store, her thoughts drifted, revisiting one of the many fights she had with Christopher when their son was small.

"I don't want people calling him Alex," Christopher had insisted.

"It's his name. We can't very well change it when he's two years old," she'd argued.

"Do you think I need a constant reminder of him*? Do I deserve to have your affair rubbed in my face every time I say my son's name?"*

"Do I deserve to be reminded of your *affairs?"*

"Maybe you do."

"You're such an asshole, Christopher. I can't believe I moved out here with you. I can't believe I let you convince me that things would be different."

"Don't say that, Abigail," he'd said, softening his tone. *"It is different. I slipped. I was still processing everything. We're good now. I promise. I just can't call our son Alex anymore, knowing that it's an homage to* him*."*

She didn't have the strength to keep fighting her husband, particularly when there was truth tangled in his words.

She'd considered changing her son's name for a brief moment when Christopher suggested, *"We'll call him by his initials instead. A.J."*

"Okay," she quickly agreed.

They never spoke about their son's name again—or about the name's intentional attachment to Joshua Alexander Stone.

Abby turned right out of the aisle just as her son's female friend was turning left toward them. Jane had gone in a circle with her father. Now, the four of them were locked inside a frozen fascination with one another.

Jane and Alex were no longer concerned with the awkwardness of running into one another outside of school. They were much more captivated by the way their parents had gotten stuck in some sort of time-stopping vortex.

"Abigail," he finally uttered.

"Hi, Josh," Abby whispered.

Chapter 2: A FORMER CONQUEST

He stepped in closer toward her. It was barely controllable, his need to get in close enough to breathe her air. He didn't want to control it, not yet. Not until he got a hit of her scent.

His head shook back and forth before the words came out. "What are you doing here?"

Jane flicked a glance at Alex, who continued to watch the interaction unfold with a perplexed expression. His neck retreated into his shoulders like a turtle shrinking into its shell.

"At Costco?" Abby replied. "I'm shopping, just like you."

Josh held her stare, unfazed by the other shoppers who were beginning to express their annoyance at having to manoeuvre around the group. His eyes narrowed, and yet somehow still managed to light up for her at the same time.

"In Halifax, I mean," he said.

Abby pressed her lips together. She wasn't prepared to unpack the last sixteen years right there next to the frozen aisle. "I could ask the same of you."

"I only ever went back out west briefly," he said. "I took over the shop after my uncle died."

"Right," she nodded, her stomach tightening. That time in her life was still hard to look back on. She tilted her chin up in search of A.J.'s face, half-expecting to see her toddler. But there he was, nearly grown, towering.

"So that's Alex, huh? All grown up, I see," Josh observed.

"You know him?" Jane blurted, yanking her head back.

Josh glanced over at Jane. "Oh," he said. "Um, no, not really. I remember when his mom had him, is all." His eyes went knowingly back to Abby.

Jane made a face like a bad odour had spread amongst them. "Weird," she said. "I'm gonna go find Mom."

"I'm gonna go get…the stuff we need at the back of the store," A.J. added, already turning away.

Abby opened her mouth to stop him. She was sure they'd gotten everything they needed. She was sure she was ready to leave the store altogether, with or without purchasing the items in her cart.

"Abby," Josh breathed.

Hearing him exhale her name, in the sultry, familiar way she remembered, sent a warm tremor through her core, like an earthquake only she could sense.

"It's good to see you, Josh. You look well." She regretted it immediately—an opening for him to return the compliment. Instinctively, she pulled her cardigan tight around her thirty-eight-year-old body, shifting from one foot to the other.

"You're stunning, as always," he said without missing a beat. "Happy belated birthday."

"Um, thanks," she replied shyly, blushing when she glanced away.

He searched for his next words. There were so many things to say and not enough time to say them. Nor was Costco an appropriate place to fawn over his long-lost love. He could sense her pulling away. She hadn't physically stepped back yet, but she was subtly searching for an out, a way to disengage from him.

"This is crazy, Abby. We're both in Halifax. Are you living here again? Are you just visiting Grace?"

Abby's mouth clumsily slipped open. She'd hoped Grace wouldn't come up. She couldn't tell him here, in the centre aisle of a wholesale goods warehouse, that Grace had been gone for nearly ten years.

"I've been living back here for a while," she admitted.

His eyes dropped to her left hand.

"Christopher and I got divorced," she offered before he could ask.

"Oh," Josh said quietly, his mind racing.

"Alex flies out a few times a year to spend time with his father."

"That's…good," Josh managed to say.

"It would appear that our children know each other," she said, scratching only the surface cause of their tension.

"Jane is my…stepdaughter." Josh paused before he said quickly, "I'm not technically married to her mom."

Abby nodded.

"I raised Janey with Andrea. She had her *after* I left Edmonton, but we did, um, get back together…after you moved." His head fell, unable to find her eyes again until the words landed.

"Oh," Abby replied.

"Can I…I mean, can we…I'd like to see you again, Abby. We should catch up."

Behind him, Abby spotted Jane again, this time with her mother. The resemblance was unmistakable. Though Jane had beautiful jet-black hair thanks to her Asian heritage, and Andrea was fair-haired with an even fairer complexion, both women walked with the same poise.

Abby felt herself shrinking.

"I don't think so, Josh," she said, continuing to monitor over his shoulder. "It was nice to run into you, but I really should be going. I've gotta find A.J."

"A.J.?"

"Alex," she corrected. "He goes by A.J. now. You know kids. The initial thing sounds cooler," she lied, scrambling to get away from Josh.

"Don't go yet," he pleaded. "It's been such a long time."

She smiled because she had already decided to leave. Relief crept in as Jane and her mother approached, making it impossible for him to follow.

"I've got to go, Josh. Take care."

Andrea placed a hand on Josh's shoulder as he was still watching Abby walk away. "Who was that, babe?" she asked casually from behind him.

Josh quickly wiped the dazed expression from his face, preparing himself to greet his partner as if he hadn't just been in a star-crossed exchange with a former lover. "No one," he lied believably. "Just someone I knew years ago."

"Oh," Andrea mouthed. She was more interested in the potted plant she'd added to her cart than the woman who had fled from Josh's proximity and never looked back.

"It was only a matter of time before we ran into one of Dad's old conquests," Jane commented.

Josh's eyes flicked to Jane carrying a light caution.

"Oh really?" Andrea perked up. "Is that true, Josh? Do you often encounter old girlfriends at Costco? Is that why you usually prefer to come here alone?" Her tone was playful, but there were hints of insecurity detectable in her light-hearted laughter.

"I prefer to come here alone because it generally saves us a few hundred dollars," he replied, staring insinuatingly into their cart of mostly unplanned purchases. "And anyway, Janey seemed to be quite familiar with the son, why don't you ask her about *that?*" Josh stuck his tongue out teasingly at Jane away from Andrea's eyes.

"Who was the boy, Janey?" her mother asked immediately.

"We go to school together, but he was nobody, trust me. I was just being nice. He's in Model U.N. for chrissakes."

"Hmm," Andrea acknowledged. She sent a knowing glance to Josh, smiling at him as they steered toward the checkout.

Josh continued to watch for Abby in every direction until they had driven far away from the store toward their craftsman home in Terrence Bay.

* * *

There were only five minutes left in their television show and Andrea was still awake. She rarely made it through an entire episode when they watched TV in bed. She must have had something on her mind that was preventing her from falling asleep. Undoubtedly, it was the same thing that was weighing incessantly on Josh's mind.

He was praying that she wouldn't ask him any questions after the show. He was in no position to offer his musings on the plot because his attention had been elsewhere.

For the entirety of the episode, as Josh sat up in bed, with one arm familiarly placed over Andrea's shoulder while she nuzzled into his chest, he'd been recalling everything he could about Abigail Conrad.

He was surprised at how effortless it was to restore old memories that had been dangling in the distance of his mind. From the time they met, over twenty years ago, to their doomed affair, to her standing in front of him in Costco of all places, just hours ago. Every memory he'd stored away of Abby kept resurfacing, unbidden, like an untamed oil strike.

No sooner had the credits appeared when Andrea asked, "So, are you going to tell me about your friend at the store?"

Josh had an important decision to make. It wasn't as if Andrea didn't know about Abby. Though they'd managed to avoid several big details surrounding his past with the Conrad sisters, Andrea always had an understanding that Josh was tethered to someone else in a way he'd never be tethered to her. He wasn't quite ready to admit to her now that the woman in the store today was the very woman at the other end of that rope. Fragile as the strand may have been after sixteen years of silence, his reaction to seeing Abby, his carnal instinct to move in next to her and take up space near her, was proof that their bonds were still intact.

He didn't want to lie either. They'd had ten good years together on the other side of a not-so-good year that nearly ended everything. At the time, Andrea's infidelity felt like karma. He sensed she'd been unhappy and he didn't blame her. He didn't do anything to improve it either.

When they first got back together, after Arthur's funeral, Josh had defaulted again to being distant, drinking more than he should've to excuse it. He would often think of the ways that he hated Abby and the part of his heart she continued to hold, even though he'd told

Andrea that, this time, he would give her more. He thought of the ways that he never actually hated Abby at all. He'd just loved her so intensely for so long, that sometimes it felt like hate. Part of him held onto hope, much longer than he should have, that he and Abby were just in one of their off-again phases.

As he got older, further into adulthood, and further into parenthood, he knew he had to accept that Abby wasn't coming back into his life. But it was too late. Andrea had already been getting the things Josh wasn't giving her from someone else. When he found out, he wasn't all that surprised. It was as though she wanted to get caught. She wanted to see Josh feel something again. It was enough of a wake-up call to snap him out of his drunken delusions about the life that could've been with the woman who was never his.

Josh cut back on the booze and called Daniel Markham.

Working with Daniel was something he knew he could pour a lot of passion into because Daniel's work was always so innovative. Josh hoped that reinvigorating his work would reinvigorate his life with Andrea. Daniel convinced Josh to partner the carpentry shop with his architectural firm, and together they created MarkhamStone.

The success of the business bolstered Josh's new outlook on his relationship, and the reconciled couple had been on a fairly smooth sail since. Of course, Janey's adolescent stages kept them on their toes, but they were able to form a united front against their teenage tyrant.

"It's nothing to worry about, hon. Just saying hello to someone I hadn't seen in forever," he answered. "I'm surprised you're still awake."

"Mmm," she purred. "Was it an old flame?" Andrea pressed.

"I dated her sister for a bit," Josh admitted, knowing that omitting relevant facts wasn't much better than lying.

"I see," Andrea responded, clearly a bit relieved.

Josh leaned over, kissing Andrea lightly on the forehead. He could see the relief in her eyes and knew she was only able to find it because she knew bits about Grace and bits about Abby. But she never knew that they were sisters. "You get some sleep. I'm gonna go out to the shed for a bit. If I lie down now, I'll just start snoring and keep you up."

"You sure you don't want to stay?" she suggested.

"I've got to get those pieces cut so I can repair the deck stairs. The weather is supposed to be dry this weekend and I want to get it done."

"Alright," she breathed with a forgiving sigh. "Suit yourself."

"Goodnight, babe. Love you."

"I love you too, Josh Stone."

Chapter 3: A JARRING RESPONSE

April 26th, 2025 – Halifax, NS

Abby jolted upright as she woke startled and sweating from a terrible dream. It had been years since she'd had a nightmare about Rob Ashford. Her fists were still closed, still gripping onto the sheets like they were the earth underneath her clawing fingers on that horrific night. The heaving of her chest subsided as she took in the safe surroundings of her unlit bedroom. Shadowed outlines of photo frames and her familiar furniture helped anchor her to reality.

Despite the lasting scars of her trauma, including that night with Rob, Abby managed her emotions by recalling that her life now was much better than it had been over half her life ago. Back when nightmares like the one that she just had were reminiscent of her present rather than her distant past.

It wasn't lost on her that the trigger for such a nightmare was Josh. Running into him, as intoxicating as it may have been, was never going to serve as a subtle nod to her former life. Reminders like that, of him, dredged up unpleasantries that liked to hover over her and occasionally plunge toward her with enough force to shatter any pleasurable recollections of Josh. The dream wasn't really about Rob. It never was.

Visions of Rob often surfaced when Abby challenged the limits of her emotional endurance. She dreamt of him when she first moved to British Columbia with Christopher after leaving Josh for good. She dreamt of him again a few times during the long messy divorce that followed five years later.

When she heard in 2017 that Rob Ashford had died of an overdose, she thought his death might finally quiet the part of her that still braced for him. Dreaming of Rob was the furthest thing from Abby's mind when she closed her eyes earlier that evening, but it did fit the pattern.

She lay down and reached for the television remote. She fell back to sleep a few minutes later to the laugh track on an old episode of *Friends*.

Chapter 4: AN ICK FACTOR

April 28th, 2025 – Halifax, NS

Jane strutted mindlessly down the hall on her way to Bio. She didn't bring her head up from her phone while passing Alex's row of lockers, so she wasn't aware that he'd quickly slammed his metal door shut to catch up with her before she entered the stairwell.

"Jane," he said, tapping her on the shoulder discreetly.

She shirked away from his touch before speaking. "Yes," she said impatiently. They moved through the doorway toward the large corner windows on the second-floor landing. The pounding of echoed footsteps flooded the hollow stairwell.

"You've been ignoring me," he whispered.

"Yes," she admitted.

"What's going on? Nobody saw us run into each other on Friday night with our parents. Seems a bit dramatic to ghost me."

“It’s not that,” she said. “I’m more worried about people seeing us together here now.”

Alex took a step back to help dissuade onlookers from making assumptions. “Do you want to call things off?” he muttered.

The bell rang, and a few stragglers scurried past them to class. They quickly found themselves alone in the vast cement chamber.

“I don’t know,” she said. “Our parents have clearly slept together. It weirds me out.”

Alex laughed, immediately relieved that he wasn’t personally the cause of her decision to ignore him all weekend. He then went back to what she’d said. “They clearly know one another. I don’t know if they’ve slept together. Did your dad say something about my mom?”

“No,” Jane answered. “He didn’t have to. I could tell just by how dumbfounded he was. It was so cringy to watch him try and collect himself. I’ve never seen him like that. They’ve definitely had sex.”

“Well okay, so what if they have? I mean, it’s weird, but it doesn’t have to change anything between you and me.” Alex stared curiously at her, attempting to catch up with whatever it was that she was preparing to point out.

“Obviously,” she said quietly enough to thwart an echo, “Josh isn’t my real dad.”

“Yeah, so.” Alex shrugged. “You said your real dad isn’t in the picture. My dad’s not exactly father of the year either.”

“Think about it, Alex. My dad said he knew your mom when she had you. My parents have never been super forthcoming with me about the timeline of their relationship. What if Josh is actually *your* father?”

“What?” Alex jerked back. “There’s no way. Why would you even think that?”

He'd never seen her this committed to one of her theories. She usually dedicated this level of over-analysis to contemplating what would happen if people found out about the two of them sleeping together.

"There's something about the way they were behaving around each other," she said. "Didn't you sense it?"

Alex recalled his instinct to shrink when his mother and Jane's father froze, how helpless they looked while they were face-to-face. There was an energy swirling around them, even there in the middle of the store, that felt overwhelmingly isolated and exclusionary. Alex had never felt so much like an outsider while standing that close to his own mother.

"I don't know," Alex said, shaking his head, shaking the confusion from his mind. "Maybe there's more to it," he admitted, "but he's not my dad."

"How do you know?" Jane pressed.

Her insistence was so irritating that Alex reached into his pocket and pulled out his phone. He opened the photo app and scrolled back to a few pictures he had from New Year's Eve in B.C. He'd flown out after Christmas to spend the remainder of his holiday with his father and stepmother, Rachel. She insisted on snapping a photo of Alex and his father in front of the tree and sent it to Alex the next day, saying, 'told you' to enforce her idea that Alex had all but morphed into his dad since being with them earlier that summer.

The two men looked nearly identical in their black T-shirts in front of the twinkling Christmas tree.

Alex held the screen up to Jane. "This is how I know."

She bent closer to inspect the image. He saw her eyebrows shoot up when she realized her hypothesis had been debunked.

"Damn, your dad's hot," she said softly, still fixed on the photo.

"Is that a compliment?" Alex asked. "It doesn't feel like one."

"Okay," she began, withdrawing from him slightly, "maybe I overreacted. My dad is definitely not your dad."

"Glad we got that settled," Alex mumbled.

Chapter 5: A RECOGNIZABLE RELIC

She fell back down on top of him, spent and sweating. He instinctively wrapped his arms around her back and, as had become their post-coital custom, Alex placed a light kiss on her head.

Once their breathing steadied, she slipped off him, wrapped herself in the silk robe on the chair in her room, and walked down the hall to the washroom.

Jane reentered the room, fluffing her long black hair with her fingertips at her scalp. "That was a good one," she announced, traces of exasperation still clinging to her voice as she climbed back into her bed beside him.

"I'm happy you're pleased," Alex replied.

She wasn't about to compliment him twice, so she simply smiled in his direction before reaching for her phone on the nightstand.

"Are you going back to school?" he asked.

"Yeah," she answered while scrolling. "I don't want to be here if my parents come home."

“What made you so sure they’d be out of the house? We’ve never come to your place before.”

“My dad has a shop out back here, and sometimes he comes and goes. He was going on about some big delivery he had to make this afternoon and I figured he’d be tied up most of the day.”

“You said before your dad’s a carpenter?”

“Yeah, pretty much,” Jane answered. “He and this guy, Daniel, run a business together. Daniel is an architect and my dad builds custom furniture for the houses that Daniel designs.”

“Oh, cool.”

“Why are you being so nosy?” Jane asked, breaking her stare from her phone screen to glance over at Alex.

“I dunno. Just curious about my *almost dad* I guess,” he said with a smirk. Though underneath his teasing, and now that the urgency he entered Jane’s home with had subsided, Alex began to take note of an odd sense of familiarity with his surroundings.

“Ew,” Jane muttered. “You can’t say shit like that right after we have sex.”

“Sorry,” Alex laughed.

“What does your mom do, anyway?” Jane asked, despite having gone back to scrolling.

“She’s an interior designer. She’s got a big thing going on with a client today too.”

“Hm,” Jane quietly acknowledged.

Alex sat up straight before turning his body to place his feet on the floor. As he dressed, he began cataloging the aesthetic details of the room. The natural wood tones of Jane’s classic and well-crafted bedroom furniture, and the wooden items that lined her dresser—a cedar keepsake box and a carved wooden horse—triggered fuzzy recollections from his childhood.

Even the colour palettes of Jane's house, what he'd glimpsed as they raced to her bedroom, felt warm and inviting, like his own home.

Alex often wondered what his house looked like when his mom had grown up there. He knew his parents had been married there, that his Aunt Grace had lived there until she got sick. After she died, everything seemed to unravel at once. His mom finalized her divorce not long after, and before he could fully understand what was happening, they were on a plane headed back to Nova Scotia.

They hadn't brought much with them. Suitcases. A few boxes. The rest had been sold or left behind.

Except the chair.

The oak rocking chair had followed them west years earlier, and then back east again. Abby had been adamant about that. At seven, Alex hadn't understood why an old wooden chair mattered so much. He'd assumed it was sentimental in the way adults were about things tied to babies and bedtime stories.

The chair had moved rooms with him over the years, upstairs when he was little, downstairs when he wanted privacy. It sat mostly untouched in the corner, except for the rare occasions his mother would sit in it when she needed to talk about something serious. She'd run her fingers along the arms, like she was remembering something.

When Alex saw the same chair—same curved runners, same carved detailing along the back—sitting in the corner of Jane's bedroom, something inside him tightened.

"Where did you get that chair?" he blurted, standing to fasten his jeans.

Jane glanced over. "I don't know. It's been around forever. I think my dad made it." She pressed her lips together in a thin, unyielding line.

"Oh," Alex replied.

They were back in his car a few minutes later. Alex kept his eyes on the road and his hands on the wheel. Jane flipped through Instagram posts in the silence. They barely spoke as he drove them back to school.

Chapter 6: A SHARED INTEREST

April 28th, 2025

Josh followed the men within an almost alarming proximity as they transferred a long, live-edge dining table from the shop to the back of a large moving truck. He watched while they covered every inch of the table with thick blankets, taping it down securely before turning it over to rest on its surface. He'd sourced the perfect walnut slab from a friend who ran a specialty hardwood shop in Bedford.

Daniel had spent two years designing Ethan Charles's immaculate home in Purcell's Cove. The dining table was one of a dozen signature pieces built custom for the house at Ethan's request, but it was by far the one that Josh was most emotionally attached to. The symbolism of a dining table, a space where people shared meals, time, and stories, gave Josh an appreciation for the life that would be lived around this distinctive, yet ordinary piece of furniture. Josh had only seen photos and renderings of the house at various stages of the development. Today, he insisted on being present for the delivery of the table that he'd built.

"Have you talked with anyone at the house today?" Josh asked his assistant, Devon.

Jumping down from the back of the truck to land on the MarkhamStone parking lot pavement, Devon said, "I've been emailing the designer's assistant, Morgan, who's been coordinating everything since the structural design was finalized. Ethan is out of town quite a bit."

"Someone will be there when we arrive with the table, then?" Josh confirmed.

"Yeah, Morgan will be there. Morgan is always there. The table is one of the last big pieces to go in the house. I think Ethan is going to be there too. He hasn't seen his own house in over a month."

"What does this guy do for a living?" Josh inquired.

"Show business, I'm told. Don't know much beyond that." Devon followed Josh back into the shop, scurrying behind him and checking e-mails on his phone. He only looked up from his screen when he had to dodge equipment and other obstacles on the way to Josh's office.

"How is it that I know more about the client than you do?" Devon asked suddenly from the doorway.

Josh searched for something hidden amongst the papers on his desk. "Daniel's the schmoozer. I just build," he said.

"Right." Devon scoffed teasingly. "The weight of artistic talent."

"As long as you keep flirting with the designer's assistant, I'll get all the information I need," Josh said.

"I wouldn't exactly call it flirting," Devon lightly protested. "I'm a professional."

"I'm cc'd on most of those e-mails, Devon. If that's not flirting, I can only imagine how you communicate with her in person."

"Who said Morgan is a 'her'?" Devon winked.

Josh glanced up with one eyebrow raised. Devon didn't seem nearly as burdened by the adult part of young adulthood as Josh had been back then. His assistant seemed to enjoy a revelry in the young part that Josh and everyone around him at the time were forced to fast forward.

Josh chuckled. "Fair enough."

* * *

Abby tucked her phone into her back pocket after reading another email about the house. The landscapers had been late, the window treatment designers had to recut a section of the large shades, and the chandelier had been damaged during shipping.

All crises seemed to be under control with the help of her dutiful assistant, Morgan. When Abby read that the statement piece for the grandiose main level had been loaded onto a truck and was on its way to the house entirely as planned, she breathed out a sigh of relief.

She continued to dart in and out of each room, inspecting the details as if they could have changed from the last time she set her eyes on them. All of the artwork was still hung straight, and the pillows were still fluffed to perfection. The day began with no less than a dozen people scurrying about the property at any given time. It was now almost three o'clock, and that number had gone down to just two after the internet technicians had completed installation of the fibre-optic Wi-Fi.

Morgan met Abby near the kitchen as they approached one another from opposite ends of the house. "The table is on its way," he announced. "That's the last thing for today."

Abby glanced over at the studded tan leather chairs that were waiting off to the side near the southern wall, ready to surround the piece that would anchor the style intentions of Ethan Charles' new home. "I just saw that. I can't wait to see it in here. This entire floor was practically designed around that table. It's going to look amazing."

"Do you want me to stick around to make sure everything goes smoothly?" Morgan asked.

"I'll be fine if you want to take off. I'm surprised you're not going to linger for a chance to talk to Devon."

"Honey, I've moved on. That man ain't nothing but a tease."

"Aw, that's too bad. I wonder if Mr. Hamstone knows that he employs such coquettish staff."

"Don't feel bad for me, boss. I've got a date tonight. I should have said I'm moving up instead of moving on."

"That's the spirit," Abby laughed.

"Can we circle back real quick to Mr. Hamstone? Is that some sort of joke I'm not in on? Or are you really walking around thinking that MarkhamStone Studio is run by one guy named Mark Hamstone?"

Abby felt her face flush crimson. She never inquired into the details of the architectural firm. She'd met Ethan after the house blueprint had been finalized and understood that the firm managed the construction of the home and all of the large custom pieces within it—like the walnut dining table that was on its way at that very moment. She must have tuned out the firm's name every time it was said, and now she burned with embarrassment over her ungracious gaffe.

When she heard the metal jingling of a delivery truck roll-up door on the other side of the entryway, Abby ran out of time to wallow in her blunder.

"Imma sneak out the back if it's all the same to you," Morgan whispered, leaning into Abby's cheek for an air kiss before he scuttled into the yard. "The house looks fabulous. Give Ethan my love," he added, his words echoing in a trail behind him as he twirled his finger above his head.

"Have a good night, Morgan," Abby called out after him.

"Did I miss Morgan?" Devon asked, waltzing into the home with his chin pointed out, bringing his sharp jaw to a perfect point.

"Afraid so," Abby answered. "Hello, Devon."

"Good afternoon, Abigail. To what do I owe the pleasure?"

"I wouldn't miss this delivery. It's the central piece of the house. Ethan is flying in tonight. He's so excited."

"It is fantastic," Devon agreed.

"How many of you are there? Do you need help getting it in from the truck?"

"Don't be silly," Devon told Abby. "You're far too precious to be hauling furniture around. Josh brought me and a couple of apprentices from the shop, so there's plenty of muscle."

"Who did you say?"

"Josh," Devon repeated. He cleared his throat before saying, "Mr. Stone. The *Stone* in MarkhamStone. He insisted on being here for the delivery, considering he built the thing."

Abby's feet went numb first before the numbness proceeded to race up through her body. She steadied herself, willing her body not to betray her.

"Oh," she finally uttered.

"You haven't met Josh yet?" Devon guessed. He leaned in closer, as if relaying a secret, "You'll love him."

"I'm sure," Abby whispered.

Chapter 7: A PERFECT FIT

She watched as his back entered the house first. His strong, solid shoulders sturdily braced the weight of the table's front end while he carved a path through the entryway. He took small, incremental steps closer to her, his arms locked and secure. He didn't know she was there, waiting to be noticed by him, terrified at the thought as he advanced further into the room.

Abby sensed she may have been discovered when he glanced back to ensure his course was clear. Her head tilted down as her lips shook like an unstoppable cold ran through her. He hadn't spotted her yet; he had only glimpsed enough to know that a person took up space near the kitchen.

"How are we doing?" Josh called out. "Is here good, or do we need to come over more?"

Devon had joined the other three once they'd made it past the threshold. Now, the four of them stood in the vast area between the sitting room and the kitchen that had been saved for the table. Their limbs wavered slightly as they struggled to keep the colossal item hovering above the wide plank maple floor before it could be set in place.

"Um, about three feet …closer to me…should do it," Abby said hesitantly.

She watched as recognition struck him. His chest expanded before he led the others in the direction she dictated. They set the table down with collaborative precision, the crossed iron legs barely making a sound when they gently touched the hardwood below them.

He didn't look back right away to confirm what he knew. He deliberately stalled the inevitable turn of his body toward hers. What if he'd been wrong? What if the voice he thought he knew so well wasn't Abby's, and the woman waiting a few feet behind him was someone else? Someone sent to tease him, to toy with his emotions, which had been desperately seeking signs of her since they ran into each other a few days ago.

"Perfect," Devon announced before heading toward the collection of chairs. "What do you think?" he asked Abby.

"You were right," she said softly. "It's a perfect fit."

"Nicely done, boss. It's wild that you two have never met. She designed a thing, you built it, and now here you both are, bringing your baby home together," Devon said. "Abby, meet your carpenter on demand, Joshua Stone. Josh, this is the home's interior designer, Abby Bouchard."

He slowly turned. His bottom lip drooped open as if speech had been lost. His eyes roamed over her without discipline in the same way they used to when they were alone together, ignoring the outside world.

Josh subtly traced the edge of his mouth with his tongue. He finally released himself from the spot that had anchored him since hearing her cadence purr in his ear moments ago.

Her torso leaned slightly back as he got closer, though her feet stayed put where she stood.

"Nice to see you again, Abigail," he said, extending his hand toward her.

"Oh, my bad," Devon declared. "You two *do* know each other."

"Hi, again," Abby breathed out in little more than an anxious whisper. She placed her hand in his and felt him grasp onto her tenderly, sliding his thumb along the back of her palm before slowly releasing her from his hold.

"You're the designer," Josh said, unsure if he was asking a question or attempting to prove what had already been revealed.

"You're the carpenter," Abby stated. She stared into his face, locked in an intimate gaze that she didn't have the strength or the desire to break from just yet.

"And I'm the assistant who is catching a ride back to the studio with Joey and Carlos in the delivery truck," Devon announced.

Josh craned his neck toward Devon, who, with the help of Joey and Carlos, had just finished placing the twelve dining chairs around the table.

"Okay," Josh agreed. "Thanks for your help. I'll see you tomorrow."

"Bye, Abby," Devon called out, trailing the other two men as they left through the front door.

Glancing away from Josh for only a second, she replied, "Goodbye, Devon."

The ten-foot horizontal hardwood pivot door swooshed closed, leaving Josh and Abby alone in the sudden quiet.

It was the first time they'd been alone together in sixteen years. She recalled the way they said goodbye to one another that day in his apartment. The way it started as goodbye, briefly turned toward forever, and then ended with goodbye nevertheless.

Seeing him the other day, with his family, in public, was like a fever dream. The world swirled around them, reminding her that there was more to the world than Josh and Abby. She wouldn't give herself the time or the luxury to contemplate meaning in the reemergence of Josh. It was too surreal, too dangerous, too intangible to begin to dissect, so she'd spent the weekend immersed in work to avoid intrusive thoughts of Joshua Stone. She redirected her thoughts, the ones within her control at least, on this house, on pleasing the man who owned this house. Never once imagining that she'd be standing in this house with the man she was trying to forget.

"Fate has a funny way of bringing us together," Josh said, interrupting their time-lapsed recollections.

A small smile crept along her lips. "I always got the feeling it was fate that kept us apart."

"How long have you been on this project?" Josh asked.

"A little over a year," she replied. Then, she offered quietly, "I didn't know that you were the Stone in MarkhamStone."

"It never even crossed your mind?" Josh asked, disbelieving.

She answered, "No," recalling her earlier embarrassment.

"I suppose if I'd have looked a bit more into Forever Sunset Designs, I would have found you at the helm. It never occurred to me that you'd move back to Halifax."

"I didn't think you were still here either," she meekly admitted.

For a moment, they stood frozen in place and time.

"Can we sit?" Josh finally wondered aloud.

"Um, I guess so," she said, glancing behind him at the sitting room. "Are you…staying for a little bit? Is everything alright with the table? I could…show you the house if you want."

"No, Abby," he interrupted. "I mean, yes, the table is fine. You can show me the house later. I want to sit down for a second…and talk to you. Don't you think we should talk? It's been forever. Seeing you twice in the span of a few days after not seeing you all this time has to mean something…doesn't it?"

"Maybe," she said. "Come with me."

She led him past the table and into the great room where they sank onto Ethan's expensive sofa. The long, cream linen sectional spanned the inner perimeter, closing in on a dark marble fireplace. Josh sat himself a respectable distance away from her, which surprised Abby. He leaned back into the couch's deep bench, stretching one of his muscular arms along the channel back cushion, his solid triceps pushing against the seam of his black T-shirt.

She was nervous and couldn't hide it. She'd been nervous since first seeing him in the store. While actively avoiding thoughts of Josh, she became inadvertently consumed by the fact that there was a likelihood she'd see him again, fearing he could be anywhere. Never wanting to be caught off guard by him again. Well, that plan failed miserably. When he arrived at Ethan's home, she was definitely caught off guard. They'd been sharing the same space now for over ten minutes. Her breathing still hadn't returned to normal. She had to move her body in overtly conscious ways to compensate for the old irregular rhythm of heartbeat and breath that struck up within her each time he was nearby.

He wasn't exactly nervous, more so uneasy with knowing they only had a finite amount of time together, but he was enjoying himself. He'd been filled with electricity all weekend, his own body like lightning in a bottle after seeing her on Friday. The possibility of running into her again, knowing they were in the same city, revitalized him in a way he hadn't experienced in years. How long had she been back, he wondered. Had running into her like that really been a possibility for years?

The kids knew each other. That was something that would take some getting used to. At night, when the house was quiet, and he lay in bed awake, while everyone else was asleep, while Andrea's slumbering breaths echoed softly beside him, it wasn't the connection their kids shared that Josh went back to. It was Abby. It was only her, seeing *her*.

He'd been drowning in her all weekend, and here they were alone, in this big, beautiful house. It was over sixteen years ago that they were in a similar predicament. Alone in a house that neither of them owned. Buried in uncertainty and tension. Holding onto one another on a white shag carpet, like the one underneath their feet right now. That was right before the end.

He could see that she was apprehensive. She sat straight and tense. Did his charms not work on her anymore? Maybe he'd been with Andrea so long that he simply wasn't charming anymore. All he wanted was to see her smile. Not a grin, not a smirk, he needed her lips to curl up in the way that made her eyes soften and let him in just a little bit. He couldn't handle anything more than a little bit, but he was practically begging for a fraction of any piece of her that just might still be his.

He shook his head, juxtaposing the joy he got just from being beside her. "I don't even know where to begin."

"Maybe we shouldn't," Abby proposed. She uncrossed her legs and placed her palms on her knees like she was preparing to stand.

"Does it trouble you to see me?" Josh asked.

She unconsciously crossed her legs again. "Not exactly. It is difficult seeing you," she disclosed. "Does it trouble *you* to see *me*?"

"No, Abby. I'm…still in shock, I think. A good shock. A welcome one."

"Shock is a good way to describe it," she said, glancing down at the section on the sofa between them.

Josh followed her eyes. "Do you want me closer or further away?"

"Neither," she answered. "Stay right where you are."

"Yes, Ma'am."

"Do you know Ethan?" Abby asked suddenly.

"Who's Ethan?" Josh asked, making a show of not caring to hear the answer.

"The client," Abby stated. "This is his home."

"Oh, right," Josh said. "No, I don't know him. Never met the guy." He turned his head from side to side before concluding, "Nice place."

He locked his gaze on her once more, preferring that sight to any of the opulence surrounding them.

"Very funny," she quipped. "You did a beautiful job with the pieces you built. The table is remarkable. Ethan will love how this place came together."

"Good. I'm glad you think he'll like it." Josh dismissed the notion as quickly as the words left his mouth. "Are you finished here? Can we get coffee or something? A drink?"

"I need to be here when the client arrives, Josh. I'm presenting his finished home to him."

"What time is that? I'll bring you back. Let's go talk somewhere else. It's a bit strange being with you like this in someone else's house." He was sure to catch her eyes when he said, "It brings back a very specific memory."

Abby jerked back and rose to her feet. “We’re not in this house like that, Josh. We’re adults. We’re…professionals.”

“I believe we were both at *that* house in a professional capacity as well,” he reminded her.

The last thing Abby needed was a reminder of what they’d done in the home she staged before she left Halifax. She didn’t need to be reminded of how he touched her that afternoon, how all she had to do was breathe out the tiniest hint of surrender, and there he was, consuming her, doing everything her body begged of him. Everything and more.

A disconcerting heat flushed through her. “It’s different now.”

“It doesn’t feel that different,” he said, his voice low.

“Stop it, Josh,” she whispered, nearly begging. “We’re not regressing into our old selves, and we certainly don’t have time to dig up the past. It’s been nice seeing you again. Knowing that we’re in the same city, and that our work creates a potential for our paths to cross, is an interesting development, but I’m not the same girl I was back then. You’re not the same guy. This was a happy coincidence and nothing more.”

Josh stood and slowly approached her. “I’m sorry,” he said. “I didn’t mean to upset you. You’re right. Our lives are different now.”

“You’re the one who’s married this time,” she pointed out.

“I’m not married,” he corrected.

“Technicality,” she stated firmly.

Chapter 8: A THIRD WHEEL

Fifteen minutes later, the heavy swoosh of the front door interrupted their chatter. Josh and Abby had somehow migrated toward the island in the kitchen. He stood on one side, his palm casually planted on the veiny marble surface. She was a few feet away, arms crossed but smiling. They'd been talking about the kids, which seemed to be a safe topic.

When it made a soft opening sound, their eyes darted toward the door at the same time to see Ethan Charles slowly entering his house in a curious state of amazement. He walked toward Abby, smiling with one hand tucked into the slim trousers of a tailored grey suit.

Sliding sunglasses atop his slicked-back dark blonde hair to inspect the finer details of the open interior, Ethan announced, "She. Is. Stunning!"

He approached Abby with far more familiarity than Josh preferred bearing witness to. Sliding his arm around her lower back and pulling her closer, he then removed his other hand from his pocket and placed it on her bicep when he leaned in to kiss her lightly on the lips. "The house isn't so bad either," he murmured near Abby's face before pulling away.

She allowed the kiss, not giving too much in return, but showing no signs of resistance toward the gesture.

"Ethan," she exhaled heavily, "allow me to introduce the carpenter, Joshua Stone."

Still holding onto Abby, Ethan quickly extended his arm to initiate a friendly, albeit solid, handshake. "Fantastic work. Really great." He glanced at the table behind Josh. "There's the pièce de résistance," he said. "You know, when Abby here dreamt up this live-edge masterpiece, I have to admit, I didn't quite have the same level of enthusiasm for it. I mean, as you can see, there's wood everywhere. I thought I wanted more of an industrial vibe, but she managed to convince me that the long lines of the different hardwoods mixed with the natural colours and textures would create a timeless look that could last decades." Ethan stared down at Abby before looking back at Josh. "I don't really know what all that means, but it's obvious that she was right." His eyes went back to Abby. "You're a genius, babe." He quickly added, "You're both geniuses."

"It does look great," Abby said, smiling faintly. "The table, the house."

"I should get going," Josh announced. "Let you get acquainted with your new home."

"Nonsense," Ethan said, his voice echoing around them. "I insist you join us for a celebratory glass of champagne. You two were instrumental in the completion of my new home. The fact that you're both here calls for a celebration."

"Josh is a very busy man," Abby timidly told Ethan.

"You'll stay for one drink, won't you?" Ethan asked in a way that wasn't really a question.

Josh deliberately caught Abby's gaze before saying, "Yeah, why not?"

"Wonderful. Darling, will you fetch the stemware while I change out of this monkey suit? I presume Tori has my closet set up?"

"Yes," Abby said quickly. "She was here on the weekend unpacking and organizing your things. I'll pour us some glasses."

"God, I've missed you," Ethan whispered, before kissing her cheek. "Excuse me for just a few minutes. I won't be long."

She moved through the kitchen with a new rigidity that had set in. She could almost hear Josh's thoughts. His judgement. His jealousy. It wasn't ideal, having Ethan put their relationship on display in front of Josh before she had the chance to tell him, but perhaps it would deter whatever plans were forming in his head, telling him they could jump back into each other's lives with ease.

"So, you're dating the client," Josh provoked.

"You're one to talk," Abby whispered harshly, her back still to Josh as she reached for a glass on a high shelf in the cupboard. "I was *your* client when we met. So was Grace."

"Technically, your parents were the clients. That's a bit different, isn't it?"

"Same principle," Abby replied, arching on her tiptoes in heels and still barely grasping the base of the flute.

He strode up behind her, reaching effortlessly for the glass she sought before placing it on the counter near the hand she had splayed on the surface for leverage. The entirety of his torso surrounded her. Abby carefully lowered her arm as he retrieved two additional glasses. She went stiff with fear. Fear that he'd sense the electric current racing through her. Or the shiver induced by the tickle of his breath landing on her neck. Fear that Ethan would enter the kitchen of his own home to see Josh pressed up against her while she silently prayed that he would do more.

She imagined herself bending at a slight angle and hiking up her skirt for him. Her throat tightened. Her chest heaved. She ached to turn and face him, eager to know if he was enraptured in a similar fantasy. The closeness was clouding her senses, lowering her inhibitions. Torturously testing her restraint.

He casually backed away, and she sank back into reality, her breath uneven, her body still caught between instinct and the woman she had become.

"How long have the two of you been seeing one another?" Josh asked from a less dangerous distance.

"About six months," she answered, pouring champagne that had been chilling in the fridge.

"Is it serious?" he pried.

"What if it is?"

"Is that your way of telling me it's none of my business?"

"What if it is?"

They locked eyes, as if they were about to engage in a Western quick-draw shootout. He squinted a little tighter; she squinted a little tighter.

"Do you love him?"

"That *is* none of your business."

"If you did, you would have said yes."

"You're a bit old for 'gotcha' games, aren't you, Josh?"

"Seeing you has made me feel young again."

"It'll pass," she said as she spied Ethan, sporting chinos and a linen shirt, on his way back down the stairs to the kitchen.

Chapter 9: AN UNGRACEFUL ESCAPE

He followed the couple from room to room, concealing exasperated sighs each time Ethan felt compelled to gush about Abby's talents, or the profoundness of a piece of overpriced art.

She overcompensated for Ethan's dramatics, turning up the dial on her professional flair like she was hosting a private viewing for an off-market listing.

They wound up back in the kitchen, filling their glasses with champagne once again before circling the table that had brought them all together. Ethan sat at the head while Abby and Josh flanked his sides across from one another. Josh had spent the better part of an hour observing how the two of them interacted. He continued to regard her now as she broke out of her formality to inform Ethan of some small lingering tasks. The taps in the pool house bar still needed to be installed. The shades in one of the guest rooms were being resized.

Josh searched for signs from Abby. Something that referenced a memory the two of them shared. Perhaps a secret glance that lasted longer than it should. She was different with Ethan than she had been with Christopher. She wasn't anxious or unsure. She didn't fear what he might say. Josh expected her behaviour around Ethan to mimic how she was with her ex-husband, or in the early days when they were together around Grace or Rob.

Josh wasn't feeling connected to her, like he was in secret back then. He felt himself wanting her, that was indisputable, but he didn't feel her wanting him back.

It occurred to him that perhaps Abby didn't need to be rescued anymore. Not from her predator boyfriend, or her sister, or even her drunk, misogynistic husband. She was self-assured in a way that he'd never witnessed before. Even the way she moved was new—like her sense of belonging in her skin had settled. He'd always seen this potential in her, sometimes overshadowed by other people, or the tragic events that plagued her adolescence, but to Josh, her magnificence was always there. It was as if she'd finally recognized it within herself. As she spoke with seasoned authority about her work, sliding back into her seat and crossing her legs with a confident command over Ethan, Abby was nothing short of spectacular.

"Of course, the chandelier situation could have been a lot worse, but we were able to salvage it," Abby remarked.

"Tori will take over, babe. Your job is done. And done quite well, I might add. I can't wait to spend a few weeks here this summer once the show wraps and things slow down."

"How long are you in town for now?" Josh asked.

"I fly back out to L.A. on Saturday," Ethan answered. "Gotta seal the deal with the network for another season. Or two, god willing."

Josh deliberately avoided asking him questions about his work because he could sense Ethan's hyperactive desire to respond to them. He sprinkled references to his Hollywood connections in nearly every sentence that crossed his lips, but Josh wasn't biting. He had a pretty good idea of which television show he must have been involved with, given all of the local media coverage a certain Netflix series that often filmed in various areas of Halifax's South End had been receiving over the past year. This wasn't the type of person Josh would usually acquaint himself with. MarkhamStone had been known for having some high-end clients, particularly in recent years. Of the ones he'd met, Josh was generally able to find some commonality between them and himself. So far as he could tell, the only thing Josh had in common with Ethan Charles was his taste in wood.

And women.

One woman.

"You're going to love it here in the summer," Abby said. "You've got such a great space out back for hosting."

"Shall we co-host a summer soirée to seal my introduction to the neighbourhood?"

"Co-host? Are you living here?" Josh asked Abby rather abruptly.

"No," she answered quickly. "I think Ethan just wants to take advantage of my address book so he can get in with all of his neighbours. I've designed a few of the homes in this area."

"It's not for lack of trying," Ethan cut in. "I keep telling her this place is not meant to be a bachelor pad." Turning his head to Abby, he smiled while saying, "Tell me you've given it some more thought at least. There's plenty of room for you and for A.J. Even though he's going to live on campus in the fall, he could still be here at the house anytime. Don't college kids still come home on weekends to get their laundry done?" he joked, sipping from his champagne.

"A.J. can do his own laundry in residence," Abby said. "I have thought about it, and I'm just not ready to leave my house. I can't stand the thought of anyone else living in it."

"You're back at the house?" Josh blurted.

Abby nodded.

"Do you and Alex live there with Grace and Travis?"

"Who's Alex?" Ethan asked.

"A.J." Abby corrected.

"You two know each other?" Ethan determined aloud, seemingly to himself, now that Josh and Abby were exchanging words between only each other. "I didn't realize that you knew one another outside of the project."

"He used to date my sister," Abby explained, still not glancing away from Josh, knowing he hated it when she minimized the degree of their acquaintance.

"But he doesn't know?" Ethan asked quietly of Abby.

"Doesn't know what?" Josh snapped.

Her mouth turned down, and her shoulders fell like thick liquid pouring downhill. Abby held his desperate glare as her face fell heavy in a way that expressed what she wasn't yet able to put into words.

"When?" Josh demanded.

She told him, "In 2015. It came back. It was quick."

"Ten years ago Abby? You never thought to tell me?"

"I feel like I'm missing something here," Ethan interrupted.

"What was I supposed to do, just call you up?"

"Yeah," Josh said before sighing to a pause. "I can't believe she's gone."

"I'm sorry," she whispered, knowing it wasn't enough. She held onto his helpless stare and felt her own eyes grow glassy and full.

His face went pale. "Me too," Josh said, aware of the unease now simmering amongst them. Wanting to avoid further discomfort, he insisted, "I really should get going." He stood to address Ethan and Abby. "Thank you for the drink and I do hope you enjoy your home, Mr. Charles. I'm sure Daniel will be in touch."

His hand found the back of her chair as he stopped to focus on her with the force of twenty years of feelings behind his eyes. "Abby, I'll see you around."

Ethan bowed his head, acknowledging Josh's desire to exit without protest.

Abby listened as his heavy steps approached the door. She didn't turn to watch him leave. She stared straight ahead, out past the deck and the yard, at the Atlantic Ocean as it lightly rippled throughout the cove. She didn't see anything in front of her because she was still so overcome by Josh. His face still lingered in her mind's eye in front of her, his eyes still begging her to give him more. More of an explanation, more of her vulnerability, more of herself. She was in no better position to do that now than she had been at any time in their lives previously. And yet all she wanted to do was run after him.

The door closed and the hum of his truck's engine faded once he turned right out of the driveway, making haste away from Ethan's home.

"I hate that you're upset," Ethan finally said, placing a hand over hers on the table.

"I'm sorry," she offered, clearing her throat to try and claim back some composure. "I obviously wasn't expecting to see him. It's always difficult to tell people about Grace."

"I can only imagine," he sympathized. "Another glass?"

"No, I don't think so. I think I'll need to head out soon."

"You'd make me spend the first night here alone?" Ethan pouted.

"You need to get used to it," she insisted. "You need to make this place your own."

"You know very well that I want to share it with someone. Not someone," he corrected himself, "you."

"Maybe someday, Ethan. You said it yourself, my job here is done."

"Your job as the designer, Abby, not as my lover."

He'd uttered the words so convincingly that she considered staying. She considered kicking off her pumps and approaching him, knowing he'd barely require any additional encouragement before he'd plop her onto the nearest convenient surface. It would be thrilling, and it would feel good, but at some point during their exploit, she would be reminded of Josh. Maybe she'd glance at the table he built, maybe she'd smell his scent lingering in the house, maybe she'd find herself wishing it was Josh on top of her instead of Ethan. Either way, she knew her mind and her body would crave him instead of the man sitting beside her now, and that was a slippery slope to embark on.

She knew she had to go. She needed to separate these men back into the corners of her life where they belonged. She needed some time to get Josh out of her mind so that she could continue her relationship with Ethan.

"Rest tonight," she told him. "Tomorrow we'll do dinner here. I'll cook. We'll test out your new appliances."

"What if I get lonely?" Ethan pushed.

"Call Tori," Abby said. "She's at an Airbnb less than ten minutes away if you need anything. She's got all the info for your tech setup and the security system. She's got your schedule for the week. You need to have a chat with her anyway."

"That's not exactly what I meant."

"I know what you meant, Ethan. The truth is, I've been working like crazy, you've been working like crazy, you've been flying all day. Let's both take twenty-four hours to rest and freshen up and we'll have a lovely evening here tomorrow. Sound good?"

Ethan leaned in closer to Abby, palming her jaw as he tilted her head so their eyes could meet. "Look around, babe. You can literally convince me of anything." He kissed her slowly to remind her what she was turning down.

"Good," she said, trying not to sound breathless. "I'll see you tomorrow." She pecked him on the cheek before pulling out of their embrace. Abby collected her purse along with a few other bags near the kitchen before heading for the front door.

"You're killing me," he shouted after her, one hand teasingly clutching his chest.

"You'll thank me tomorrow," she called out, blowing him a kiss from the foyer.

She began on the winding road toward the city centre roundabout that would link her back to Clayton Park, but Abby didn't make it two minutes out of Ethan's driveway before eyeing a man outside of his truck near the North Star Yacht Club. The truck was unfamiliar, and the man had been for a time as well, but in reality, no amount of time could pass in which Abby would forget the way that Joshua Stone appeared alongside a Ford.

She pulled her Tesla onto the curb and came to a stop behind him.

"An electric car? Really?"

"It's new. It was Ethan's idea. It's growing on me," she explained. "Someone's got to counterbalance all the emissions from that beast."

"I remember a time when you were quite fond of my truck."

"Times have changed. I've changed."

"I can see that."

"What are you doing, Josh? Is something wrong with your truck? Why have you pulled over here?"

"I was waiting," he answered.

"For who?"

"For you."

"How did you know I'd leave so soon after you?"

"Just a hunch." In truth, he needed to collect his thoughts and the first place that had a shoulder wide enough to pull onto with close access to ocean air seemed like a good place to do so. There was part of him that hoped she'd follow him out.

"Don't be smug," she warned him.

"How do you want me to be, Abby?"

She shook her head and shrugged. "I don't know. I thought there would be more…distance between us if we ever saw one another again. I thought maybe someday I'd pass you on the street and we'd smile at one another, but we'd both keep going. Maybe one, or even both of us, would glance back, but that would be it. I never imagined you'd just turn up and insert yourself into my life again."

"That's quite a delusion you've crafted. Did you ever think that maybe it's you inserting yourself back into *my* life? I've been here all along, Abby. You're the one who came back. Did you never think to look me up?" he challenged. "Obviously not, considering you didn't even have the decency to tell me about Grace."

"I'm sorry," she said, surrendering a bit as she approached him. "Of course I thought about looking in on you and your life. I didn't have the courage to find out anything about you. I thought it would be better that way. I thought you hated me. By the time I came back, when Grace was sick, I had already left Christopher. I didn't call you because I knew if I did I'd only end up throwing myself at you in a very unhealthy way, and…" she said, trailing off at the end.

"And what?"

"And you would have let me," she finished.

"Why would that have been such a bad thing? I could have been there for you."

"Running to you then wouldn't have helped me grieve Grace, Josh. It wouldn't have helped me grieve my failed marriage. It wouldn't have helped me grieve…losing you."

"You never had to lose me, Abby."

"Josh," she uttered breathily, "I've been losing you in one way or another since the day we met."

Chapter 10: AN OBVIOUS QUESTION

Two hours later she was alone in her kitchen. Lit by only the lights above the island and a small lamp in the living room, Abby drank chilled white wine and watched her memories perform around her like scenes in a play.

She saw herself eating cereal at the island the day her mother told her to keep watch for a visitor:

"Mom, your camera," Abby called through a mouthful of cereal as Debra fumbled at the door.

"Oh god." Debra snatched it up, capped the lens, and stuffed it into her bag. She kissed Abby's cheek. "Joshua Stone will be here around one. I'll bring something home for dinner. Love you!"

The door slammed shut. Abby looked at the empty room and muttered, "Who the hell is Joshua Stone?"

She watched as a teenage Josh guided two young women through the front door moments after they'd just learned that their parents were dead in a car crash. With compassionate hands wrapped around both their shoulders, he led them to the sofa where he held Grace and Abby as they sobbed and slipped into an uncertain silence.

She heard her young voice back at the island and glanced over to see herself and Josh again, the day he finally told her what he'd been holding in for years:

"Abigail... if I say what I'm about to say, you won't be able to unhear it."

"Will I want to?"

His pause was long, tortured. "I honestly don't know."

She sank onto a stool, gripping the counter like an anchor. "I'm listening."

He inhaled sharply, words tumbling out. "All the reasons I've kept quiet about my feelings for you, I don't believe in them anymore."

Her eyes shifted to the seat beside her own, where Josh had been sitting on that explosive Thanksgiving:

Grace shoved her chair back and stood. "Oh, Abby," she cried, hand to her chest, "tell me what it's like to have a knight defend your honour."

Rob looked around, confused. "Am I missing something?"

"Ask them." Grace gestured at Abby and Josh, then stalked to the island, gripping the counter edge with both hands, knuckles white.

Josh scowled. He couldn't help it, his eyes went to Abby.

"Don't look at her," Grace barked. "Don't you dare look at her."

"Leave her out of it," he snapped, pushing up from his chair. "You want a fight? Fight with me!"

She spied her paralyzed frame in the space preceding the kitchen the day he reappeared in her life, before her wedding, without warning:

Her heart stalled.

Josh Stone. In her kitchen.

Every version of him that had ever lived in this house flashed at once: the boy barefoot on the tile, the teenager laughing at the sink, the young man standing exactly where he stood now.

He finally pulled a water bottle from the shelf, twisted the cap, and took a long drink. When he lowered his head, he saw her. The entire world shrank down to the narrow distance between them.

Though Abby had lived a lot of life since the day the twenty-year-old version of herself stood frozen in front of Josh, she felt very much the same way now. Helpless disbelief, yearning for the impossible, anxious about the inevitable, all of those paradigms had become current again, like a retired trend that was catapulted back into style.

Just as another recollection threatened to surface, Abby realized this time it wasn't a memory—it was real life walking past the entryway.

"Hey Mom, what are you doing?"

"Hey bub, nothing really. Just relaxing."

"You looked like you were completely zoned out."

"I'm just tired."

"How did it go at Ethan's?"

"It went great. He loves the house."

"I didn't think I'd see you tonight."

"I didn't foil any of your plans to have a girl over, did I?"

A.J. laughed before answering, "No, Mom, nothing like that."

Abby smiled at her son, completely charmed by him, as she was sure any girl would be. With his father's good looks and the alluring Conrad disposition (that Abby was certain had somehow skipped her), A.J. oozed a quiet charisma. She didn't like to get too involved in her son's romantic life. He got his first serious girlfriend in the tenth grade, who proceeded to give him his first broken heart before Christmas of the eleventh grade. Since then, he'd kept mum about his affairs.

"I've got some reading to do before bed," he told her, walking closer to his mother to squeeze her shoulders.

She glanced up at him, "Okay, I'll see you in the morning."

A.J. went to the fridge to get a drink on the way to his room. Turning back before disappearing down the hall, he posed, "Mom, can I ask you something?"

"Of course," Abby replied.

"You know the rocking chair in my room, the one we brought back from B.C.?"

Abby inhaled, nodding unassumingly through her exiting breath. "Mm-hmm."

"Where did that come from? It always seemed like it was pretty important to you. Did it belong to my grandparents or something?"

"No. It was built for you, for your nursery actually," she answered with caution.

"Built by who?"

"A family friend," she told him.

"Was it Jane's dad?"

"Why would you ask that?"

"She told me he was a carpenter."

"I thought you barely knew her," Abby pointed out.

"That's beside the point, Mom. You're avoiding something."

"As are you, Son, so it would appear."

"How well do you know Jane's dad?" he pressed her.

"How well do you know Jane?" Abby retorted.

"I'm serious, Mom."

"Me too, kiddo."

A.J. slowly approached the island, resting a hand on the surface while he assessed with a quizzical stare just how evasive his mother was behaving. "I'm seeing her, if you must know. Not seriously or anything. We're not even technically dating."

"If you're not dating her, then what *are* you doing with her?" Abby asked reflexively, though she quickly understood what the answer would be.

A.J. shrugged his shoulders; a self-satisfied expression on his face said everything he didn't.

"Oh," Abby acknowledged. "Don't you think it's a bit insensitive to keep things that… one-dimensional?"

"Don't meddle, Mother. We're both happy with our arrangement."

"If you say so. Just be careful," she warned her son. "Not in the 'use protection' way, although please, for the love of god, use protection, but also remember there are feelings involved. Hers *and* yours."

"Now that I've told you my secret, are you going to tell me yours?"

"It's not a secret per se," Abby said. "It's just never come up before."

"I'm asking you now," A.J. urged.

"Asking me what?"

"Mom!" he scolded. "You know exactly what. How do you know Jane's dad? Did he build the chair?"

"Yes, if you must know, he built the chair," Abby finally confessed. "He built your crib as well. I think it's still in the attic." She swallowed, saying more seriously, "I used to know him fairly well. He dated your Aunt Grace when we were teenagers."

"Oh," A.J. uttered.

"Josh lived here at the house with us for a little while when your grandparents died. He…helped us sort out our lives after we lost them. Grace and I didn't know what to do. We didn't want Uncle Tom or anyone moving in to try to take the role of our parents. Grace was eighteen and figured we could make it on our own. Josh…helped." Abby clung to the last word, knowing that her selective explanation of Josh was intentionally deceptive. She hadn't lied. She'd chosen her words carefully because she wasn't ready to tell the whole truth.

"So he was Aunt Grace's boyfriend?"

"Yeah," Abby answered, "at that time."

"And what happened? They just broke up and he moved out?"

"Sort of."

"That sounds…incomplete," A.J. surmised.

"Aunt Grace met Uncle Travis soon afterward. Josh had moved away. I met your dad. And that was that."

"But he said he remembered when I was born. Why was he around when I was born if Aunt Grace was already with Uncle Travis?"

"Oh, um, well, he did come back right around the time I married your father, the first time Aunt Grace got sick." Abby hated that she was weaving a false narrative for her son, the same one she once used against herself.

"He still had feelings for her?"

"Not exactly."

"Mom, did something happen between you two? Jane thinks that it did."

"You've talked about it with Jane? What did she say? Did Josh tell her something?"

"No. I don't think so anyway. But the two of you did seem to be… caught up in something when you saw each other."

"It's complicated, honey."

"Uncomplicate it for me. I can take it."

"It was a long time ago, A.J. Things were very different back then when Josh was in my life."

"So, he was more than just one of Aunt Grace's boyfriends?"

She hesitated before answering, "Yes."

"Were you in love with him at some point?"

Abby felt compelled to tell her son the truth after he'd worked so hard to coax it out of her. "Yes."

"While you were with Dad?"

"I won't do this," Abby sighed. "I'm not about to sit here and dissect my marriage to your father with you. Your dad and I didn't work out and we're both happy now. We're finally at a place where we can co-parent with some civility and we're so proud of you, A.J. I know you understand more than you probably should about the problems we had. But you don't need to know anything more about the role Josh Stone played in my life almost twenty years ago."

"Okay. Okay. You win," A.J. said in surrender when he saw the toll it was taking on Abby. "I'll leave it alone." He walked to her once more and kissed her on top of her head, saying, "I love you, Mom. Goodnight."

She watched him disappear down the dark hallway. "Goodnight, sweetheart."

PART 2: YOUNG LOVE

Chapter 11: A FINE FORM

May 2nd, 2025

Alex was in one corner of a crowded house. Jane was in another. Their eyes had met a few times throughout the night, but they hadn't spoken to one another. It was part of their arrangement. They didn't interact openly at social events. No one from school could know they were involved. Though Jane had lost sight of why it mattered so much.

Alex left his group of friends to get a drink. There was a large collection of half-filled liquor bottles on a round table in the kitchen and a stack of red solo cups on the counter. He eyeballed a long pour of rum into the plastic, staring fascinated as the echo dulled with the rising liquid level. He helped himself to a can of Coke from the fridge and added half to his drink then took a sip, wincing as the alcohol seared his throat on the way down. He instantly swallowed a second mouthful without recovering from the first.

Jane strolled into the kitchen as he was motioning to exit. He held up his drink so that she had space to navigate past him in the narrow entryway of the old house. She stopped as their bodies were pressed against each other with small crowds on either side of them.

"Hello," she whispered near his face.

"Hi," he said back lazily.

"You're in fine form tonight."

He raised his eyebrows curiously. "Have you been watching me?"

"No," she lied. "It's just obvious."

"Why is my form any concern of yours? We don't really know each other, do we?"

"Is that how it's going to be?"

Alex chortled. "I didn't make the rules, Jane. I'm simply playing by them."

"Maybe I don't want to play by those rules anymore," she confessed through a whisper.

"This is news to me."

"Can we go somewhere and talk?" she asked.

"We're talking right now," he pointed out.

"Somewhere private," she insisted.

"I thought we had new rules."

"Please," she urged genuinely enough that he felt obligated to follow her up the stairs.

They found an unoccupied room. Dinosaurs and Star Wars artifacts stuck out to Alex each time his eyes permitted focus as his gaze clumsily shifted direction.

Jane sat at the foot of the bed while Alex remained standing unsteadily before her. She reached for the waist of his jeans, gripping either side of the button, ready to undo it.

He put his hands on her forearms. "What are you doing?"

She scoffed. “What does it look like I’m doing?”

“I actually thought you wanted to talk.”

“We can talk afterward.”

“No, Jane,” he said in a moan that went against his objection.

“Fine, we won’t talk afterward.”

“We don’t need to hook up tonight,” he told her.

She jerked back, staring up at him. “Why not?”

He wavered, mumbling unintelligibly, “You’re drunk. It wouldn’t be right.”

“Piss off, Alex.”

He tugged on his pants and took a small step back to release himself from her hold. “I mean it,” he said with more composure. “We don’t need to do this tonight. Not here. I don’t even know whose fucking house this is. This is a kid’s room. Where’s the kid?”

“Relax,” she instructed, sinking back further onto the bed. “This is Harrison Thornton’s house. His family is away for the weekend. I’m assuming they have Harrison’s little brother with them.”

“Oh,” Alex replied with notable relief. “How did I miss that?”

“It probably slipped out of your brain three rum and Cokes ago.”

“We should get out of here,” he suggested.

“Why are you trying to get away from me? You haven’t messaged me all week. We haven’t talked since Monday.”

“I’ve been busy. I had two assignments due this week.”

“I thought you were *coasting til graduation,*” she mocked.

“I still have to hand stuff in,” he replied.

Jane asked blankly, “Are you done with this? With us?”

He answered truthfully, “I don’t know.”

“What don’t you know?” she snapped back.

“I don’t know if this makes sense anymore since it’s not gonna go anywhere.”

"Why do you think it's not going to go anywhere?"

"You've been too ashamed to admit that you even know me for starters."

"That's not true," she weakly refuted.

"That's entirely true."

"Well, that's what I was going to talk to you about," she said. "What if you took me to prom? We could announce that we're official that night."

"Oh," Alex gasped, theatrically putting a hand to his chest, "could we? That would be so cool. Think of all the likes you'd get if we went offish at *my* prom."

"It was just a thought," she sulked. "You don't have to be so rude."

"I just find it sort of ridiculous that you want to turn my prom night into a spectacle about you. You'll have your own prom next year. Besides, you already know I'm taking Sarah. We decided to go to prom together ages ago."

"Are you really still planning on going with her? I thought she was just a fallback."

"No," he corrected, "she was always going to be my date because that's what her and me agreed to."

"What? Are you, like, in love with Sarah?"

"I'm not in love with anyone," he declared harshly before realizing how hard his words had landed.

"Oh," she whimpered.

"Jane," he began, "this isn't a surprise to you. This…we…you and me…we were just having fun…right?"

"Yeah, I guess."

"I didn't even know you were thinking about telling people. I assumed you'd ghost me as soon as school got out."

"Me too," she agreed.

"What changed?"

She sat up straighter, quickly faltering when she met his eyes.

Carefully, he asked, "Do you…have feelings for me?"

"Are you stupid?" she cried out quietly.

"I don't know," he answered slowly. "Maybe."

She quietly asked him, "Do you have feelings for me?"

"Yeah, of course. I care about you a lot, Jane. I wouldn't have been doing this if I didn't."

"What changed?"

"Nothing's changed. I still care about you. I guess I just didn't think you cared all that much about me so I made sure not to get too invested. The fact that I'm going to college in the fall is getting more real. And now there's this weirdness of our parents knowing each other."

"I thought you didn't care about that," she snapped.

"I don't care that much. It's just…when you add it to all of the other stuff…" he said, trailing off. "I'm trying to be realistic."

"I don't care anymore if our parents know about us."

"You seemed to care last weekend," he recalled.

"I could feel you pulling away this week and I realized that I don't want you to. There. Are you happy? I said it. I, Jane Barrington, might be in love with you, Alexander John Bouchard."

"Might be? Are you sure you wanna do this, Jane? You'll probably wake up tomorrow with the same amount of disdain you've always had for me."

"Stop," she said, standing to approach him. "I'm serious. I am in love with you. Do you need some sort of gesture to believe me? Do you want me to go shout it at the party downstairs?"

"No," he replied, lightly laughing and shaking his head.

She put her hand on his chest to disarm him and leaned closer, placing her lips in front of his, then swerving to whisper, "Don't you want me?"

Before he could answer, her mouth was grazing the side of his face, trailing his jaw. She kissed him like she was trying to prove that she meant it, like she could inject her intentions into him this way.

He received the kiss with slightly less vigour, wrapping his arms around her waist to hold himself steady while she reached up behind him clutching fistfuls of his hair. When she went for his waistband again he backed away from her, knocking a Baby Yoda action figure off a white dresser onto the light blue carpeted floor.

"I think we need to revisit this with clearer heads," Alex blurted.

"I promise I'll still feel the same way tomorrow," she said breathily.

"Sleep on it," he instructed. "I'm gonna walk home to sober up. Make sure you get home safe, okay?"

She stared at him, wanting to test his resolve further, but ultimately wanting to gain his trust more. "Fine," she conceded. "Will you message me when you get home?"

"Yeah," he agreed quickly before kissing her cheek and exiting the room.

Chapter 12: A PORCH SWING

May 3rd, 2025

It was close to one o'clock in the morning when Jane crept through the front rooms of her house, trying not to disturb her sleeping parents.

She stopped at the fridge for a bottle of water and saw from the kitchen window the faint light of her dad's workshop at the far end of the lawn. Listening closely, she could hear the dull hum of rock music playing inside.

Jane moved slowly through the short grass of her backyard and crossed the small section of cement in front of the open red lacquer door. She stood at the entryway unnoticed as Josh used a sheet of fine-grit sandpaper to smooth the curved edges of a cut piece of hardwood.

"You were supposed to be home an hour ago," he announced coarsely without looking up.

"I know," she replied a bit startled to find she'd been spotted. "I'm sorry."

He turned the radio volume down and slowly glanced up at her as if he was waking from a dream. He wasn't angry, but there were signs of something unsaid on his face.

"You're not old enough to come and go as you please, Janey."

"You know where I was, Dad. You guys both track me on your phones."

"That doesn't mean you get to act irresponsibly. You've been drinking."

She narrowed her eyes at the empty beer bottles on the small window ledge behind him. "So have you."

"I'm an adult," he stated.

"Are you fighting with Mom?" she asked.

"No," he answered quickly, continuing to glide the paper along the grain. "Why would you ask that?"

"You're out here late on a Friday night. Drinking by yourself."

"I couldn't sleep because my daughter was out past her curfew."

"Very funny," Jane sneered. "What are you building? Is this something for work?"

He responded bluntly, "No."

"Something for the house?"

"Maybe," Josh mumbled.

"Well, what is it? Is it a surprise?"

"Not really," he answered. "It's the arm piece for a porch swing."

"A porch swing?" Jane echoed disapprovingly. "Dad, in case you haven't noticed, we don't have a porch."

"Maybe someday we will," he mumbled.

"You're weird," she declared.

Josh smiled to himself and took a seat in a worn wooden chair beside his equally shabby wooden desk. He set his project down and met his daughter's wearied eyes. "You haven't been yourself this week, Janey. Anything you want to talk about?"

She studied him, knowing that his easy disposition was either a ruse, or a result of too many beers.

She tested his disarming demeanour by asking "How did you and Mom get together?"

Josh pursed his lips while trying to decide on what he'd allow himself to share. "You've heard this story, Janey."

"Not really. Nothing specific. All I know is that you once worked in Edmonton, where Mom is from, and started dating when I was really young."

"There's not much else to it." Josh was impressed by how casually the lie escaped him.

"You're lying," she asserted.

He sat up straighter in his chair, unhappy with the change in her tone. He'd forgotten how clever she was. "You're right," he admitted. "I met your mother before you were born."

Shocked by his candour, Jane approached her father and perched on his desk beside him. "What?" she responded. "How long before I was born?"

"We dated for a couple of years before she got pregnant with you," Josh answered.

"Why did you never tell me this?"

"I guess we thought it would be easier."

"What about Grandpa? And Uncle Ben? Did you know them too?"

Josh sighed, knowing he'd already divulged more than he should have, more than they agreed upon years ago. "Yes, Janey. I knew your Grandpa and Uncle Ben before I met your mother."

"How?" she asked, still in a state of open-mouthed fascination.

"I worked for both of them. I moved out west to work on a rig that your grandfather just happened to run. I worked for Ben too so I could still do carpentry stuff out there. Your mom worked at a bar when she was in college. That's where we met."

"She's going to kill you for telling me all this, isn't she?"

"Let me worry about your mother," he told Jane. "Why are you thinking about this stuff now?" Josh leaned back, giving himself some space to get hit with the response that he feared was coming.

"I saw you with that woman. Alex's mom. There was…something there. I was just wondering if it had anything to do with Mom… or with me."

"It doesn't," he insisted.

"I'm old enough to know the truth."

"It's time to get to bed, Janey. We don't need to get into this now." He already thought himself a fool for sharing too much, and now he'd have to lie his way around this to avoid Janey finding out the truth. It didn't feel good to be a man who had to lie to his daughter, even if he believed it would protect her.

"How did Mom get pregnant with me?" Janey blurted as Josh attempted to usher her out of his wood shop garage.

One brow was lifted when his eyes found her face.

"I don't mean it like that, I know *how,* obviously. I mean when did she meet my biological father? Where were you? Did she cheat on you?"

"No," he answered. "It wasn't like that. We were broken up." He held the door open, still urging her to walk ahead of him as he continued. "I've already told you too much, but I want to make sure you don't have a misunderstanding of what happened between us. If anything, I fucked up."

"Did *you* cheat on *her*?"

"No, Janey," he said quietly.

"Then what was it, Dad? How did you and Mom date right before I was born and again right after? What happened in the middle?"

Josh went still with one hand holding the door's edge above Jane's head. He took in a full breath and then admitted after a long exhale, "I didn't fight for her. She had her reasons for wanting to leave…and I let her go."

"What about Alex's mother? You said you remember when Alex was born."

Josh did the thing he despised. He decided to twist a half-truth to downplay his attachment to Abby. He said, "I knew Alex's aunt. We met when I was still in high school and I knew his mom through her sister, Grace. It was another lifetime ago and it's got nothing to do with you or your mom."

"Oh," Jane said, tilting her head and relaxing the tense furrow in her brow.

"It's been a long day, kiddo. Time for bed."

"Okay," Jane agreed, drooping her head sleepily.

Josh reached his free hand toward the inside wall near the door, flicking the light switch off as they left the small building. The last thing he saw before the space went as black as the night was the round-edge rectangle he'd been sanding when Jane arrived. A crude sketch of the swing on creased and aged paper sat underneath the piece of pine.

A drawing he conceived over twenty years ago.

* * *

October 22nd, 2003

They were parked in his Ranger watching the incoming tide steadily overtake the rocky shore. Abigail wore a dark green knit sweater that made the flecks of gold in her eyes pop. Her hair was in a perfectly messy bun with teasing tendrils dangling inches from her mouth on either side. Her jeans had rips above the knee.

Josh caught himself staring at an exposed part of her left leg. He'd seen her many times before in shorts and swimsuits, but there was something particularly arousing about this unprotected bit of flesh taunting him beneath pitiful strings of denim. He could imagine the smoothness of her thigh below the cotton, but he dared not reach out and touch her. Her body, much like the young woman herself, was forbidden.

Of course, it hadn't stopped him from dropping everything each day that week at three-fifteen so he could be in the school parking lot by three-thirty when she was dismissed.

Grace's apoplectic performance at Thanksgiving had inserted a wedge between him and Abby that she wasn't willing to ignore, but Abby didn't want to stay away from him either. A triumphant glow radiated from her cheeks every time she spotted his truck waiting for her at the end of the day.

His mouth was getting dry inside the truck. The humid autumn air blowing between them through the open windows of his truck did little to settle him, and seeing parts of her that he could only dream of reaching out to touch made his arid words crack nervously when he finally spoke. "Are you…Is everything alright at the house?"

"I can't talk about Grace today, Josh. My sister and I aren't speaking much, but if I talk to you about it, I'll start replaying all of the things she said, and all of the things I've done, and then I'll remember what a terrible person I am and I'll realize that I really shouldn't be here."

"You're not a terrible person, Abby. A terrible person wouldn't think twice about being here with me. She wasn't thinking about you when she was with Rob. You haven't done anything other than fight against what your heart wants."

"I don't know how much longer I can keep fighting," she admitted weakly, her hands squirming restlessly in her lap.

A thick moment of concentrated silence stirred between them before he asked, "Are you ready to surrender to your heart, or your head?"

She slowly answered, "I don't know."

"How do you see us?" Josh blurted.

"What do you mean?"

"Haven't you ever thought about what it would be like to be with me?" he asked with a sultry dip in his tone.

Abby forced out an audible exhale, like she was offended at how personal the question was, then swiftly diverted her gaze down away from his. "Yes," she confessed shyly.

"What do you see when you think about us together? What are we doing? Where are we?"

"I used to think about us just like this, except you chose me in the beginning, and all of the things you've done with Grace over the years, you did them with me instead. Movie dates, dinner dates, nights hanging out at my house, or us swimming together in the pool. I used to imagine what it would be like to have Grace watch *us* from the sidelines."

"Are you still thinking about those things?"

"I want them more than I ever have. I just know that they're much further out of reach now."

"Do you ever see a time when us being together is within reach?"

"Maybe we'll run into each other again when we're older and we'll pick up where we left off."

"So," he laughed, " I just need to give you up for, like, twenty years and then we'll find our way back to one another?"

"Surely things will have settled down by then," she joked.

"Will you still be in love with me then?"

"How could I not be?" Abby answered. "The question is, will *you* still be in love with *me*?"

"Why is that the question? That should never be in question. I don't care how old we are. Anyone who comes and goes in my life from here on out is doomed to be compared to you."

"That hardly seems fair to your future wife," Abby said, sporting a devious grin.

Josh reluctantly got in on the fun. "What is your future husband going to think of me waiting in the wings for you to leave him for me?"

"He'll have to adjust," she claimed.

"So after my wife leaves me because she's gotten sick of my tireless pining over another woman, and you finally decide to get rid of your no-good husband, where does that leave us?"

"Why was my husband no good?" she protested lightly.

Josh took a second to lock into her eyes, his mouth twisted up in a hypnotizing smile as he answered, "Because he wasn't me."

"Oh," she uttered agreeably, "of course."

"Right, so what do you see now that we've gotten all of that out of the way?"

"I see us," she began, leaning back into the faded cushion of the passenger seat, "but older." Abby peered out at the Atlantic Ocean as she sketched a mental image to share with him. "We're looking out at the water just like now because it reminds us of when we were young. Maybe we live in one of those houses over there," she explained, pointing at a spot farther down the coastline past Point Pleasant Park. "The house has a big front deck and we sit out there most evenings after supper to drink tea and watch the tide."

"That sounds nice," he said longingly, contemplating the horizon while her description emerged in his mind.

"You've built us a porch swing and we rock slowly back and forth while the waves ripple gently through the harbour."

"A porch swing, huh?"

"Yeah," she sighed wistfully, "a porch swing."

* * *

May 3rd, 2025

Tired as she had been, Jane was unable to find sleep. Rolling around in her bed, thinking of Alex and the things they had done together in that same spot, on those same sheets, just days before, made the fact that he hadn't messaged her that night, or that week, that much more unsettling.

Something about the way her father expressed a sentiment that seemed an awful lot like regret had stuck with her. Her mother had her reasons for leaving him all those years ago, and he didn't fight for her. Jane's mom would have had to have spent a long time feeling unwanted for her to decide to leave Josh, just to end up pregnant with Jane soon after.

Jane couldn't stand the thought of losing Alex. She no longer cared about what people at school would think, and thought it quite possible that they didn't think about her nearly as much as she once hoped they did.

Alex clearly wasn't the sort of guy who was enchanted by aloofness. She wasn't prepared to let him go over something as stupid as feigning disinterest when the truth was that she had been falling for him long before the first night they hooked up.

There'd be no way to mistake just how serious her declaration of love was if she declared it to everyone all at once. She couldn't take it back, couldn't deny it after it was sent out into the world for all to see. Alex didn't want a spectacle at the party or a show of force at his prom, but there were other ways that she could proudly claim him as her own.

She deliberated briefly on the fact that he hadn't felt the need to make any professions in response to her own earlier in the night. Perhaps she overwhelmed him, or he wasn't thinking clearly from the rum, but she knew he felt things for her that no one else had ever expressed.

He was the only boy who kissed her with an intention purer than sex. It never felt like he was using her, despite how used to being used by other boys she had become. He held her when they were alone in a way that made her feel safe. She never worried that he'd talk to other people about the things they'd done and the ways she moved her body to please him. Maybe that was part of an underlying reason that she insisted on their secrecy. The intimacy they shared was part of the thrill. But now she'd pushed him to the point where he appeared irresolute.

Jane wasn't about to let him hold on to a reason to leave her—she had to fight for him, or risk losing him for good.

Chapter 13: A GRAND GESTURE

May 3rd, 2025

Most of the students at Halifax West High School followed Jane on TikTok. Even those who didn't out of jealous spite still managed to come across her content on their feeds. Countless videos of the latest dance trends, daily outfit selections, and seemingly strange challenges filled Jane's profile, making her the most viewed and most 'liked' student at school. A few hundred followers from other schools throughout the city also added to Jane's growing online reach.

Only a few dozen people saw the post when she recorded it live at 5:30 am in front of his house. She didn't initially see any names she recognized as they rolled along the bottom of the screen, some even leaving behind supportive heart emojis. It wasn't until closer to seven, when some of the weekend-employed members of the student body were waking, that the notifications began to stream in at a steadier pace. She didn't look at them, not yet. She was still high on the thrill of it. Jane was practically giddy with excitement as she returned home in her father's truck. She grabbed the can of white paint, the roller, and the tray, out of the truck bed, then walked them back to Josh's workshop. She was never going to be able to deny what she'd done, but still thought it prudent to return the borrowed items from where she'd lifted them hours before.

* * *

Abby's phone had buzzed a few times from where it rested near her side of Ethan's bed. Work e-mails she presumed. Until she was conscious enough to remember that it was Saturday and work e-mails didn't generally alert her with this much early morning urgency on weekends. Sleepily, she reached her hand along the nightstand. There were four text messages from her neighbour, each becoming more concerning in tone:

6:30 am: *Mark said he drove through something strange on the street in front of your place on his way to the golf course this morning. Do you know anything about it? I'll have a look when I take the dog for a walk.*

6:52 am: *Mark says his tires are a mess with white paint.*

7:09 am: *Looks like a message or something. I can see giant letters from my window. Is this another promotional thing for work that you're filming?*

A photo was attached to the final text. The smeared letters on the street were there for everyone to see.

7:31 am: *I swear each letter is about 7 feet tall. It says 'J&A 4EVER'. I thought you were still seeing Ethan! Who's the J? Am I missing something here?*

"Oh my god!" Abby uttered. She tossed the blankets from her body and shot up into a sitting position on the bed. Scrolling through her messages, this time with the utmost diligence, she hoped to find an additional notification stating that this was a misunderstanding or a joke.

Abby's neighbours, Shannon and Mark, had moved into the house beside her family home before Grace got sick again. They were a retired pair of empty nesters who had been friendly with Grace and Travis for years and thus felt a sincere obligation to keep a watchful eye on both the house and on Abby.

"What is it, babe?" Ethan grumbled beside her.

Abby jumped out of bed and began to frantically throw her clothes on. She set her phone atop a dresser with the speaker on and listened to the line going unanswered as she waited for A.J. to pick up.

"I've got to get home. Something is going on at the house and A.J. isn't answering his phone," Abby explained.

"Slow down," Ethan said, slowly rising to sit and face her. "Is everything alright? I'll come with you."

"A.J.'s tracker says that he's home. He's probably just sleeping, but I still need to get home. I have a couple of messages from my neighbour saying that there's paint on the street in front of my house."

"What, like a spill?" Ethan guessed, still visibly groggy. "Doesn't seem like that much of an emergency. I'll have it washed for you. I'll call Tori. Come back to bed."

"No, not a spill. I think it was deliberate. Shannon's husband drove through it this morning. I'll have half the neighbourhood complaining about this in the community Facebook group before lunch."

"Who would deliberately paint your street?"

"I don't know, Ethan," Abby sighed. "I'm heading home to find out. I'll call you when I get things sorted." She poked her head out of an old grey NSCAD sweater that she had been wearing on Ethan's patio last night. Bending over as her arms found their way through the sleeves, Abby kissed Ethan quickly on the lips. "Hopefully, I can clear this up in time to still ride out to the airport with you."

"Like I said, I can have Tori look into this. We can spend my last few hours together in bed like we planned. Like you promised me last night," he said pouting.

Abby had convinced herself, after a few days of turmoil, that Ethan was a safe bet. Seeing Josh again had jolted her, but she wasn't about to let him rock her universe with his unexpected encroachment on her life.

"I wasn't planning on having my street painted when I made that promise," Abby told him. "I'll call you soon," she said. "Stay in bed. I'll have some breakfast delivered for you."

"I have people for that, love. I want *you* in my bed, the *people* can get the breakfast."

"One of these days, you'll realize that you can't always get what you want."

Ethan stood and reached for Abby's waist, pulling her into him and kissing her firmly on the lips. "I got you, didn't I?" he reminded her through a husky sigh.

"Very funny," she replied, placing her hand on his chest to lightly propel herself out of his hold.

* * *

Moments later, she was racing toward the Armdale Rotary. She told Siri to dial Morgan's number. He picked up on the fourth ring, though his tone indicated he wasn't thrilled to do so.

"Sorry to bother you on the weekend Morgan, but I need a number for Mr. Stone. Joshua. The Stone in MarkhamStone."

"I know you didn't call me to get a number you could have Googled," he sassed.

"Not the studio number," she explained. "Besides, it's Saturday, I'm sure there's no one there."

"Right," he agreed. "Some people don't even talk to people they work with on weekends."

"I need a number that can get me in touch with him directly. I thought you might have it," Abby said. "Or, maybe you're friendly with a certain assistant who would definitely have his number?"

"Are you really asking me to reach out to that despicable man, Abby?" Morgan whined.

"Afraid so, and I don't have a lot of time, so if you could do it like right now, I'd really appreciate it. I'll take you for dinner next week," she offered. "Somewhere expensive. I'll let you tell me about the Real Housewives."

"Ugh, you know I'll do anything for a free meal and a chance to kiki about Erica Jayne."

"Thank you, Morgan. Call me back as soon as you can."

Abby was idling at a red light on Joseph Howe Drive when she answered Morgan's return call, unaware of the fact that all Morgan had to do was turn to his left in bed and nudge Devon awake to extract the information he'd been tasked to procure.

Abby voice-dialled Josh's number as she headed toward Lacewood Drive. He picked up on the second ring.

"Hello?" he groaned, obviously unaware of who was calling him at such an early hour.

"Why on earth would you paint my street?" she asked.

"Abby?" Josh whispered, jumping out of bed to try and make sense of this erratic call, further away from a sleeping Andrea.

"J&A 4EVER!" she called out. "Is that supposed to be some sort of joke?"

"I have no idea what you're talking about," Josh insisted, now leaning his back against the kitchen counter, wearing only his boxer briefs.

"I got messages from my neighbour saying you painted that in front of my house. Her husband got paint all over his tires this morning on his way to the golf course. I'm sure they won't be the only ones complaining. Do you know how embarrassing this is, Josh? What's A.J. going to think when he wakes up and sees this? How do I explain this to Ethan if he finds out? Not to mention your wife and daughter."

"Back up for a second, your neighbour told you I did this?"

It was the first time since she'd read what was written that she'd even stopped to consider the possibility that the culprit may have been someone other than Josh. A sharper wave of nausea hit her.

This wasn't about them. Not this time.

"Well, no, she didn't say it was you, exactly," Abby uttered slowly.

Josh took in an audible breath. "You just assumed it was me?" he laughed. He turned to face the window, glancing at the backyard and the garage off to the side. He thought he could make out that the light inside was on.

"It wasn't?" she asked, but it was more like she was ready to accept it.

"Sorry to disappoint, but no," he told her. "Perhaps we need to ask *Jane* and *Alex* if they know anything about this."

"Oh my god," Abby sighed. "Jane and Alex. J&A." She waited a moment before announcing, "They've been seeing each other."

"I know," Josh admitted.

"How do you know?" she snapped.

"She brought him to the house last week when nobody was home. I saw them on the doorbell camera. It didn't look like they were here to study."

"Were they skipping school?" Abby cried.

"I don't think that's our biggest concern right now," he reminded her.

Abby shook her head forgetfully. "Right."

"I've got a pressure washer in the garage. I'll come wash the street for you and then I'll have a little chat with Jane."

"Okay," Abby said agreeably, "Thank you."

"I'll be there in twenty minutes," he told her.

Her thumb hesitated over the steering wheel disconnect button. "I'll see you soon," she said.

Chapter 14: A TIKTOK

He returned to the bedroom, dressing quickly and quietly. Andrea stirred as she heard the familiar creaking of the floorboard by the closet door.

"What's going on?" she asked Josh.

"Nothing," he answered. "I have to run out for a bit. I won't be too long."

"Did someone call you? Is it work?"

"Not really, but I promise you don't have to worry. Go back to sleep," he urged.

"Josh," she said assertively, "why are you leaving the house at eight in the morning after receiving a panicked phone call from a woman?"

"I didn't mean to wake you," he stated.

"Answer the question," she insisted.

Josh huffed. "I don't know all of the details," he told her, standing near the bedroom door with an obvious resolution to exit. "I think it's got something to do with Jane and a boy she's dating. She may have…" he hesitated, "painted something on the street. I've got to go wash it off."

Andrea sat up, summoning a greater level of alertness. "What?" she balked. "What boy, what street?"

"I'm sure I can get it cleaned up quickly and then we'll sit down and talk to her about it."

"I'm going with you," Andrea decided.

"There's no need," Josh insisted. "Stay here and wait for Janey to wake up."

"Who called you?" Andrea asked. "How did they know to call you?"

"The kid's mother called me," he answered. "She knew that Janey and her son were seeing each other.

Andrea folded her arms and drew a breath. "There's got to be more to this."

"That's why you should stay here and check in with Janey."

"Okay," she reluctantly agreed. "Will you call me when you know more?"

"Of course," Josh said before turning to leave.

* * *

Josh inspected the driveway and surrounding area once he'd stepped outside and into the beginning of a vibrant and crisp spring morning. In placing his palm on the hood of his truck, he inferred that it wasn't as cool as it should have been for remaining stationary overnight. Now with a better vantage point, he could confirm that the garage light was left on. He remembered turning it off last night as he walked Jane into the house. She had been acting strange when she arrived home after the party, asking questions about Josh and Andrea's relationship, about Alex's mother.

He drove with a determined stillness while the speed of his thoughts matched the acceleration of his tires along a nearly barren Prospect Road.

He empathized with Janey, knowing she had become involved in something that had evidently reached a dramatic climax, but his mind was stuck on Abby. Driving toward the house that was once a temporary home, the house that had felt like home for so long, so long ago, stirred something in him that had never fully gone quiet.

Abby was outside when he pulled up. He caught sight of her in a sweater that was all too familiar, one that she'd worn more than once on chilly summer evenings when she favoured curling up in Josh's arms over her husband's. She had the garden hose pulled out to the street and was making little progress in an attempt to wash the paint away.

"Thank god you're here," she called out, shielding the morning sun with a hand to her brow.

He fetched the pressure washer from the truck bed, carrying it in one hand as he strolled toward her. "A man could get used to a welcome like that," he said, greeting her.

Ignoring him, she gesticulated toward the monstrous alphabetical display. "This is even bigger than I thought."

"That's what she said," he joked nervously.

Abby struggled to suppress a laugh while a smile played at the corners of her lips. "Apparently, it's online," she said. She'd gotten a hold of her son before arriving home to find him panicked and pacing in the driveway. "A.J. said he woke up to a million messages. Jane posted a TikTok right after she did it. The whole school knows about them now. I guess it had been under wraps before. He's doing a bit of damage control inside."

"Sounds like something they need to sort out themselves," Josh said. "But I'll certainly be having a chat with Jane about the part that my paint and my truck played in all of this."

Abby watched him get things in place and prepare to turn the machine on. Staring up at him, she felt an inexplicable closeness despite years of separation. Before the noise of the power hose would drown out conversation, Abby approached Josh and touched his arm lightly, saying, "I'm going inside to see how he's doing. I'll be back out in a few minutes."

He was able to wash the paint quickly. A few cars slowly passed him, their drivers staring bewildered at such an unexpected sight as they swerved to avoid Josh.

Abby came back outside as Josh was returning his pressure washer to the back of his truck. Her eyes darted first to the newly cleaned section of street and then up at Josh. "Thank you," she said sincerely.

"It came off pretty easy," he assured her.

"I'm sorry about all this," she said. "I shouldn't have called you like that. I shouldn't have…blamed you. I shouldn't have let my feelings cloud my judgment."

Josh shifted his balance, placing his arm along the edge of the truck bed as he stood facing her next to the driver's side door. "What do you mean?" he asked. "What feelings?"

"You know what I mean, Josh. I don't need to spell it out for you."

"Maybe you do," he insisted. "I was under the impression that our reintroduction into each other's lives was somewhat of an inconvenience for you."

Abby felt the bubble around them sealing. The vacuum that formed anytime she was alone with Josh for too long. Like they were the only two people in the universe. Like divine intervention was intervening just for them.

"Just because you weren't in my life for all these years, doesn't mean that I stopped caring about you," she confessed.

"Likewise," Josh echoed.

"Neither of us is at liberty to…express anything further," Abby stated, knowing she'd said too much, having already released a heap of untamed emotions toward him.

He stared intensely down at her; his narrowed eyes said what he knew he couldn't. She was right, he couldn't say anything else without triggering a butterfly effect series of events that could have impacts on a whole new generation.

But maybe it already had.

They were standing outside of this house, not reeling from a dinner with Grace gone wrong, not bickering about the complications of their lurid affair; they had been brought together this morning because their children had somehow made it into each other's lives in a very consequential way. Had they already dragged their children into the wreckage they never cleaned up?

From her peripheral, Abby spotted a black Porsche SUV slowing down before it came to a stop directly behind Josh's truck.

He glanced back when he saw Abby's attention get redirected.

"Oh shit," he mumbled.

"Who's that?" she asked.

"That's Andrea's car."

"Josh and Andrea," Abby said quietly. "J&A 4Ever."

Chapter 15: A POWERFUL TSUNAMI

Jane exited the passenger side first. Andrea emerged from the driver's side a few seconds later. Josh could discern from where he stood that Jane had been crying. He couldn't tell yet if his daughter's tears were a result of some genuine remorse, or an effort to evade accountability for her actions. She had come to master the latter in her adolescence.

Andrea locked eyes with Josh, her chilly stare saying more than she'd dare to say in company. She had carefully surveyed the scene she witnessed upon arrival and wasn't pleased. Were the separate factions of Josh's life about to intertwine?

Andrea walked steadfastly beside Jane, guiding her toward where Josh and Abby hesitantly awaited the women's approach.

"Janey has something she'd like to say to…" Andrea paused, leaning her neck in toward Abby, hoping she'd volunteer an introduction of herself.

"Umm, Abigail. Or, um Abby is fine," she said clumsily, stumbling over her own name.

"I'm sorry Abby…err, Mrs. Bouchard," Jane murmured softly, averting her gaze from the adults crowding around her. "I'm really sorry for painting your street."

Abby tilted her head, sighing. "It's all taken care of now thanks to your dad," she replied, oozing compassion for the young girl. "A.J. is inside if you'd like to speak with him," she offered.

"Ok," Jane said. "Thanks." She took her leave, glancing only briefly in her father's direction before heading up the driveway and through the front door.

"I'm sorry about all of this," Andrea said once the door had closed behind her daughter. "I'm sure it's not how you envisioned your weekend beginning."

"I'm sorry too," Abby said reflexively.

"What do you have to be sorry about?" Andrea asked playfully.

"Why did you drive out here?" Josh blurted.

"Jane spilled the beans shortly after you left. She was mortified when her TikTok backfired. She's starting to get some backlash. A lot of people were blaming her for coming between A.J. and another girl." Andrea shrugged her shoulders and shook her head.

"A.J. doesn't have a girlfriend. Surely, he's not a cheater," Abby declared. She felt Josh's eyes on her before she'd even gotten the words out.

"I got the feeling that it was an ex-girlfriend the student body was sort of rooting for," Andrea explained. "Jane was mortified when she started to see the comments people were leaving. It's all over social media."

"A.J. and Sarah were pretty serious until they broke up early last year. As serious as you can get about someone when you're in the tenth grade anyway," Abby said, stealing a glance at Josh, her eyes lingering on him for just a moment longer than she planned. "They stayed friends as far as I know. I believe they're going to prom together."

"I think Jane may have gotten more attached to A.J. than she intended," Andrea speculated. "She admitted to being a bit jealous of the prom thing."

Abby offered no reply, simply nodding with pursed lips. She hoped that A.J. was handling himself with some humility inside. She recalled their conversation on Monday night, warning her son that his insouciance could come at a cost.

"Would you like to come in for some tea or coffee?" Abby asked, darting a glance between Andrea and Josh.

"You can head back to the house if you want. I'll wait for Jane and drive her home," Josh offered a tad too eagerly.

"Don't be silly," Andrea told Josh. "After a conversation like that, Janey will want to talk to her mom. It's best I drive her home." She aimed a telling smirk at her partner, then smiled fully at Abby and responded, "Coffee would be great."

"Follow me," Abby directed, turning to walk toward the house.

Josh reluctantly trailed behind the women.

Upon walking through the foyer, Andrea declared, "Your home is gorgeous."

"Thank you," Abby said.

"Abby's an interior designer," Josh announced once they had positioned themselves in the kitchen.

Andrea took a seat at the island, still assessing her surroundings.

The cupboard paint and handles had changed over time, but the butcher block remained. He skimmed his hand over the surface as he walked past and came to a standing stop to lean his back against the counter. Being in this kitchen flooded Josh with memories of what it used to represent. Bittersweet nostalgia swept over him like a powerful tsunami.

"Oh right, you two know one another," Andrea said, feigning a lapse in memory. "We saw you at the store last week," she recalled. "Well, this place is great. If your house is any indication, you must be very good at what you do."

"I grew up here. My parents bought it in the nineties, then my sister and her husband lived here for a while, and now it's my turn I guess. I haven't done anything major. My mom had a great eye for things. She was a photographer. Maybe that's why I got into interior design."

"It looks pretty different from what I remember," Josh noted. "Especially with the hallway wall gone."

"Yes, I suppose I'm used to that now," Abby laughed. "It did change the way the light carries through the main floor. The rest of the footprint is pretty much the same as it was."

"You spent some time here?" Andrea asked.

Josh glanced at Andrea as if he'd forgotten she was there. "A bit," he answered.

"Because you dated Abby's sister, is that correct?"

"Yes," Josh and Abby answered together.

Andrea eyed them both with caution.

Abby cleared her throat and added, "Josh went out with my sister, Grace, when they were in high school."

"You kept in touch with her, didn't you, babe?" Andrea continued. "She was at Arthur's funeral, wasn't she? I think I remember seeing her."

Abby had been reaching for mugs in the upper cabinet beside the sink. She spun after hearing Andrea's question and met Josh's loaded stare.

"Yeah," he muttered, "she was there."

"And how is she now?" Andrea asked. "You mentioned she *used to* live here with her husband. Do they still live in the area?"

Unable to prevent helpless glances from finding Josh, Abby replied, "Grace passed away. She had ovarian cancer."

"Oh god, I'm so sorry. Josh, did you know? You let me prattle on about it."

"No one asked you to give Abigail the third degree," Josh snapped.

"Forgive me," she said. "I really am sorry."

"It's alright," Abby insisted. "Not, you know, alright that she passed away. I just mean, it was ten years ago, you know. Um, so, yeah. I'm…alright." Abby caught Josh's shoulders falling from the corner of her eye. She could feel him wanting to come to her, wanting to embrace her, to protect her. "I still miss her though," she said, sighing.

An uneasy silence fell over them as Abby poured coffee into three mugs. She brought two of them to the island and went to the fridge to fetch the cream. Josh opened the drawer next to the dishwasher and pulled out a teaspoon. When Abby returned to the island with the creamer and sugar, she was startled to find him there with a spoon as if they had been coordinating their efforts.

"Oh," Abby whispered. "Thanks." She took the teaspoon from Josh.

"You seem quite comfortable in this house," Andrea observed.

He sent her a warning glare from across the island.

Abby kept her head down and returned to the counter to retrieve her mug.

Josh would deal with whatever conversation awaited him at home, but he wasn't about to let this turn into something else here. Though Andrea's aggression was passive and slight, perhaps even undetectable to Abby, it was wholly obvious to Josh and he found it increasingly challenging to mask his irritation.

Facing the couple once again, Abby summoned a careful smile. "I wonder how the kids are doing."

Chapter 16: A LAST RITE

Jane's heart raced with unsettling intensity underneath her paint-smeared T-shirt. She sat at the edge of his bed, watching Alex pace in front of his bedroom closet door.

"Are you alright?" he asked.

"This isn't exactly how I saw this going," she mumbled.

He walked delicately toward her and sat down. There was enough space between them that they weren't touching.

He rested his palms on the top of his knees. "How did you see this going?"

"I thought you'd be impressed," she said. "I thought you'd see how much I wanted to be with you out in the open and it would make you want me that way too."

"I don't know what to say." Alex shook his head.

"The fact that you don't feel compelled to tell me that you want to be with me too says enough."

"It's not that I don't want to be with you," he said gently.

"But," she interjected.

"I don't know, Jane. I want to be honest with you and I want to protect you from the fallout of all this. I don't know."

"Please tell me whatever it is that you're too scared to say."

"I'm not scared. I just think I didn't realize it until very recently."

"That you're in love with Sarah?" she assumed again.

The fall of his chest and a long blink confirmed what she suspected.

"Why bother hooking up with me?" she asked. A tightness in her throat added a vulnerable squeak to her weakening voice.

"I like you, Jane. I wanted you. I never thought in a million years that you'd be interested in someone like me, and when you were that night at Keisha's party, I wasn't going to say no."

"You just wanted to get with me because I'm popular? Funny, I actually believed you weren't like other guys."

"No, that's not what I mean. You know we exist in different circles at school."

"Do you think if we hadn't been sneaking around all this time, things could have been different for us?"

"I don't know. I knew it wouldn't have been easy for you if we went public. It was exciting to have a secret, but it let us both believe that what we were doing wasn't entirely real."

"Is that how you were able to be with me and still love her?"

"I can't talk about Sarah with you, Jane. She's…she's gotta be off limits. She's going through enough online right now."

"I never meant for her to be involved in this," Jane confessed, biting her bottom lip.

"Well, she is. Now the whole school is talking about her. You might be used to that, but she's not."

"I'll talk to her if you want. I'll apologize. I'll make another video to try and clear things up."

"I don't think you should make any more videos about this. Just let it die out," Alex insisted. "I'll call Sarah. The explanation should come from me."

"So, that's it? Are you and I supposed to just *die out* like the video?"

Alex found Jane's eyes and managed to summon compassion like a priest prepared to deliver last rites. He set a hand on top of her white-knuckle grip on his bed. "I think we have to."

Jane let the finality of his words wash over her, accepting them as much as she could while her teenage hormones and exhausted adrenaline attempted one last surge.

"I didn't want to be your Sarah. I wanted to be your Abby. But it looks like I'm doomed to follow in my mother's footsteps."

He flinched at her suggestion. "What are you talking about?" Alex asked, ready to jump to his mother's defence if need be.

"I know you see it, Alex. You'd be crazy not to."

"What happened between our parents in the past is none of our business."

"It is our business if we're just going to screw it up the same way they did," she said. "Think about it. Your mother and my father are clearly in love with each other, even to this day. I don't know what happened that made him choose my mom, or your mom to choose your dad, when they obviously wanted each other more. But here we are. Standing in the middle of it. Making them question if they chose wrong."

"That's insane."

"Maybe. Maybe it's fate."

"For who? Us or them?"

"Maybe both," Jane posed.

"Maybe neither," Alex countered.

"I don't want to lose you because of them," Jane said.

"It's not good for you to go around assuming your dad isn't happy with your mom. They've made it this long. Longer than my parents did."

"Did you ever ask yourself why your parents got divorced?"

"No, I was a kid. I barely remember them together. Besides, my dad is remarried and my mom has a boyfriend now. She seems happy."

"You're saying she hasn't been a bit out of sorts since running into my dad at the store? She hasn't seemed particularly reminiscent? Distracted?"

"I wouldn't know," Alex lied, recalling his conversation with Abby earlier in the week.

"Well, it's been written all over my dad's face. He's a terrible liar. I don't know if my mother is pretending to be oblivious or if she's detached herself from it somehow, but she won't be able to ignore it while the three of them are sitting out there in a room together. It's palpable."

"What is?"

"The fact that your mother is the one who got away and my mother was the next best thing."

His mouth hung open. "You do know how crazy you sound, right?"

"Just make sure you know which one I am before you toss me away, Alex. We don't need a crystal ball to see into our future. It's literally happening in your kitchen right now."

Chapter 17: AN ETERNAL BEACON

Jane spilled out of A.J.'s bedroom, marching resolutely down the short hallway toward the kitchen. She paused briefly, facing the adults as a wary hush fell over them.

"Mom, I'm ready to go," she mumbled.

"Okay, Janey," Andrea said, sliding her stool out to stand. "Thank you for the coffee," she said to Abby. "It was nice meeting you, despite the unusual circumstances."

"No problem," Abby replied. "Nice meeting you too."

"I'll be right behind you," Josh said, catching Janey's compunctious gaze.

Janey shrank herself once more to say, "I'm sorry again, Mrs. Bouchard."

Abby nodded kindly. "Don't worry about it."

"See you at home," Andrea directed at Josh, a subtle warning woven in.

"Hm hmm," he said, nodding. He didn't make a move to go. He silently observed as the women left the house together, leaning into one another like they'd both barely survived something.

He wanted to speak, wanted to say something real, something that didn't necessitate a decoder ring. He didn't want to talk to Abby through tone or subtext. He longed to pour his heart out to her there in that kitchen in much the same way he did when he was nineteen years old.

The bedroom door down the hall had opened again. Head down and standoffish, A.J. waltzed past Abby and Josh while they were voicelessly time-locked in memories.

"Are you okay, hon?" Abby asked.

"Yeah, I'm fine," A.J. answered, turning back to face his mother. Though he tried to hide it, a silent alarm went off in his body upon realizing that Jane's dad remained in his house. His posture straightened, his jaw flexed ever so slightly, and his hands withdrew from his pockets, one clutching his car keys.

Abby saw the two men meet eyes. Josh relaxed his disposition when he noticed A.J. firming his.

"You remember Jane's dad, Josh," Abby said cheerily.

"Yeah," A.J. said.

"He was able to get the paint off the street. He was just leaving."

"Right." A.J. cleared his throat and muttered, "Thanks."

"Are you going out?" Abby asked him.

"Yeah, I've got my phone," he told her.

"Okay," she said, backing off.

A.J. was out the door and halfway down the street in less than a minute.

A sudden brightness overcame Josh's expression. "You remember the day I babysat him while you napped upstairs?"

"He was just an infant then," Abby reflected.

"I don't think he likes me as much as he did back then."

"He's probably wondering why you're still here," she guessed. "And he's not alone."

Josh fought to conceal a smirk. "That's not very hospitable."

"Your cup is empty, sir. The kitchen is closed."

He glanced down into his empty mug before placing it in the sink beside him. Abby lingered near the edge of the island, willing him to follow her before something was said that couldn't be unsaid. The impossible words seemed to dangle right above their heads, begging to be plucked from the air and inserted into the morning.

Though he smiled at the ease with which she mimicked his playful banter, Josh collected a mindful breath and crossed his legs at the ankle as if he wanted to emphasize, rather seriously, that he wasn't prepared to leave. He wasn't willing to step out of this house, this opportunity to be alone with her. This fleeting, almost miraculous chance to take her in.

Staring at her with his mouth and eyes turned up ever so slightly, in his most unguarded condition, he said, "How am I supposed to leave here? How am I supposed to just walk out that door as if you're not here in this house, living your life twenty minutes away from where I live mine?"

"You have to," she told him. "We both have to accept that this is the way our lives turned out. You're with Andrea. I'm with Ethan."

"I can't just go home to my wife and forget you," he protested.

"I thought you weren't married," she teased.

"Technicality," he quipped.

She turned from him, shaking her head. Their witty back-and-forth was only an opener. She knew he was poised to dig deeper. Despite his wife and daughter leaving his sight mere moments ago, they were somehow a distant memory to him. Josh and Abby's past tension had been summoned to the surface, eclipsing the now. Passion overshadowed prudence.

"You really see yourself with Mr. Hollywood?" he challenged her, taking long strides out of the kitchen to catch up with her as she attempted to lead him to the door. They stopped in the foyer, facing each other again, closer this time. "Why did we meet again now? We can't be in this house together again and pretend like it doesn't mean something. I don't buy that."

"I'm not trying to sell you anything, Josh," she said. "I'm sorry I called you. I'll own that. I'm sorry I brought you back here."

Inching closer to her, forcing his hand to stay by his side while he resisted the urge to touch his palm to her cheek, he revealed, "I'm not sorry, Abby."

On the verge of tears, at the precipice of showing weakness, Abby backed away, forcing her vulnerability down and her shield up. "What do you want? I can't wave a wand and make it so that you don't know I'm here again."

"I don't want that," he huffed. He knew he'd been close. He knew she'd been seconds away from leaning into him before her old friend, fear, convinced her to pull away. "I think we should at least acknowledge that we're at a crossroad," he said. "Again."

"What crossroad Josh?" You have your life, I have mine. That hasn't changed one bit," Abby argued.

Approaching where she'd migrated into the living room, he swiftly crept around her, perching himself on the arm of the sofa so that he could face her closer to eye level. He took her hands into his, not giving her a chance to refuse his pleading touch. "Everything changes when you're in my life. Everything. Are you saying that after things settle with the kids, you're going to go back to acting as if I don't exist? You're going to go to work and to the grocery store, and anywhere else in this city as if the possibility of running into me doesn't spark even the slightest bit of curiosity somewhere inside of you?"

She'd let the weight of her hands sink into his, and though she hadn't pulled them away, because she wasn't quite ready to go back to a world where Josh Stone was not permitted to touch her, as she so achingly wished he would, she maintained, "I have to. And you do too."

He weaved his fingers between hers, pressing their palms together firmly. "I can't, Abby." His voice lost its edge. "That's what I'm trying to tell you."

"Don't say something you shouldn't," she cautioned.

He swallowed, jaw tightening. "When you're around—" He shook his head, frustrated. "Even when you're not around. It's like there's this…"

She didn't move. Didn't rescue him.

He finally said, quieter now, "I have this eternal beacon that is constantly lit for you."

He let go of one of her hands but didn't step back. His fingers traced lightly along her arm, slower this time, almost reverent.

"I can't dim it anymore," he admitted. "Not when you're close enough to see it."

A pause.

"Close enough to feel it," he whispered.

Abby allowed herself briefly to step out of the now. They were together in the past; she was in his arms. They were seconds away from making love. They'd been making love in secret all summer. She anticipated the feel of his lips landing on hers with the urgency he'd been combating for years. Until she'd finally given in. Until she'd permitted herself one night of freedom from consequence. Then one night turned into many. Then a collection of digressions caught up to her and she was forced to cut him loose.

She let herself drift for a second. Back to the summer. Back to the first night she told herself it would only be one mistake.

Were they still paying for that?

The question landed heavier than she expected.

Grace.

Rob.

Her parents.

The list formed without her permission. She tried not to follow it further.

She had always felt as though there was something to atone for. As though choosing Josh had required a kind of penance she'd never quite finished serving.

Maybe resisting him had become part of it. Maybe that was the cost.

Andrea probably didn't carry that kind of debt.

Abby did.

Finding the courage to stare into his eyes after avoiding them for fear of their intoxicating lure, Abby noticed something grab his attention out the living room window behind her. She spun her head, half expecting, in an oddly nostalgic lapse of reality, to see Grace at the other end of his glance.

A black town car slowed to manoeuvre around Josh's truck before turning into the driveway and stopping behind Abby's Tesla. Her hands slipped free from Josh's grasp with the weight of a descending anchor.

Ethan got out of the car, straightening his suit jacket before he studied the street and then the truck in front of Abby's house.

"Ethan's here," she announced, stepping out of Josh's circle, shattering the swelling aura of desire that had been threatening to consume them.

"I can see that." Josh let out a defeated sigh. "Fantastic timing," he muttered as he watched her open the door and welcome Ethan into the house.

Chapter 18: A HEAVY SHACKLE

Josh stood tall, straightening his shoulders and preparing to square off with Ethan like they were scheduled for a duel. He saw Abby exhale when she opened the door, relief blowing out from her chest toward the man who had provided it. Josh didn't want to be someone Abby needed relief from. As much as he believed they were reeling each other back into something more real than the reality around them, he soon began to understand that he was the opposite of relief for her.

He was the burden. Not the escape, but the thing she needed to escape from. The heavy shackle that dragged her back to a past so intense it would make anyone crave relief.

Abby and Ethan embraced one another in the entryway. He kissed her on the lips the way people in new relationships kiss. Like they hadn't been inconsequentially kissing each other for so much of their lives that the desire to linger in a kiss had left them entirely. Ethan was hungry for Abby. He craved her, but worst of all, as Josh watched

Ethan guide Abby's hair away from her face and behind her ear, he was almost certain that this man had genuine feelings of love for her.

The intimacy of the gesture made Josh involuntarily flex his fingers at his sides. Ethan was quick to spot him, now standing awkwardly off to the side, waiting for them to unblock the area so he could bolt. Josh's body told him to flee. To drive away and never look back; never think back.

Ethan pulled away from Abby, glancing at the motionless man in the living room. "Joshua…right?"

Josh nodded, suddenly feeling like his height was somehow oafish and unsettling. Ethan couldn't have been any taller than five ten. Josh thought he seemed like the type of guy who probably told people he was six feet tall, or wrote it on forms that asked for his height.

Glancing back at Abby, Ethan made every attempt to remain unaffected when he inserted far too much breeze in his tone to sound sincere. "Am I missing something?" He grinned, the confidence on his face clearly forced.

"It's a long story," Abby answered. "Josh kindly washed the paint off the street."

"I was just leaving," Josh said. "Good to see you again, Mr. Charles. Hope you're settling into the new house."

"I was," Ethan replied. "Sadly, I'm off again. I hope to be in town longer next time."

Josh nodded again and motioned toward the couple, praying they would clear an exit path for him.

As Josh began to approach, Ethan turned to Abby once more. "I'm sorry, but why is it that the carpenter was the one to clean the paint? I told you I'd get Tori to take care of it."

Josh recoiled, mouthing *the carpenter?* to himself while Abby began to devise a response on the spot.

"Our kids know each other," Abby told him. "It seems they've been dating…or whatever. It was Josh's daughter who painted the street. Josh offered to clean it."

"I suppose I should be thanking you then," Ethan decided, expecting a dip of his head to relay the sentiment all the same. "Will you come with me now?" he asked Abby.

"I don't know, Ethan, it's been a pretty hectic morning," Abby said. "I want to be here when Alex gets back home."

"The driver will have you back in an hour. I don't want to say goodbye to you like this, babe. I didn't want to say goodbye the way you left this morning either." He gripped her arms on either side and leaned in so close that their foreheads nearly touched.

"Safe travels," Josh interrupted, as he moved around them. He paused at the door, making sure his eyes connected with hers when he said, "Take care, Abigail."

Josh made a forceful stride onto the cement landing and faked indifference as he waltzed to his truck. His jaw locked as he crossed the lawn, knowing—and hating—that he'd left her, once again, in the arms of someone else.

* * *

That afternoon, Abby was in the backyard, back from the airport, retrieving patio furniture cushions from the shed. It was a bit early in the year to be so optimistic about the continuation of good weather, but it was unseasonably warm. A short respite in the serenity of her budding backyard might serve to improve an otherwise confounding day.

She stretched out on a lounger she'd placed beneath a large umbrella, holding her Kindle in one hand while taking occasional sips of white wine with the other. Her body acclimated quickly to the comfort. The noise from the street was almost completely dulled back behind the substantial brick home. The chirps of spring crickets and intermittent bird songs were enough to lull her into a total state of relaxation.

The light swoosh of footsteps in the brittle grass went undetected until they were almost directly behind Abby.

A woman cleared her throat to announce her presence and avoid startling a clearly unsuspecting host.

"Hi…Abby?"

Abby quickly straightened in her chair, tossing her head to confirm that the very person she feared had paid her a visit was in fact peering down at her in the shade.

"I'm sorry to barge back here like this. I rang the doorbell a couple of times. I saw your car in the driveway and the gate was open beside the house, so I took a shot."

"Oh, um, okay," Abby stammered.

"I was hoping the two of us could talk…alone," Andrea said.

Abby stood, smoothing her dress and then her hair, and feeling as though neither effort put her in a position to confidently stand so close to a woman as casually gorgeous as Andrea.

"If this is about the paint, don't worry about it," Abby said. "I hope Jane's okay. Alex seems to be alright, although I think the whole thing served to bring him and Sarah a bit closer."

"It's not about the paint, Abby," Andrea said decidedly. "Or the kids."

"Oh." Abby sighed. "Do you want to come into the house?"

Andrea observed, "It's quite nice out here."

"Um, alright," Abby complied. "How about some wine?" she asked, lifting her glass from the small table by her knee. "Do you want some Chardonnay?"

"That'd be great," Andrea agreed.

"I'll be right back," Abby told her. "Make yourself comfortable." She gestured toward the table and chair set on a cement slab area near the French doors.

Abby went inside and immediately placed her trembling hands on the section of kitchen counter closest to the door. Her head fell between her shoulders and her chin tucked into her chest as she took deep breaths to try to regain composure.

She had imagined how a conversation with this woman might go many times before. And now that woman was here. In the flesh. Sunlight catching in her hair. Effortlessly composed. Beautiful in a way that didn't try too hard—because it had never had to.

Abby felt it instantly, the old collapse inside her ribcage. The quiet, poisonous question she'd buried years ago rising back to the surface: *How could he love me if he could love her?*

It had been the same confusion with Grace. If Josh could want someone like her, someone luminous, someone obvious, what did it say about Abby? That she was the secret? The exception? The mistake?

Andrea didn't look like a mistake.

Standing that close to her, Abby felt herself shrink, not physically, but somewhere deeper. The sixteen-year-old version of herself surfaced without permission. The girl who always felt slightly off-centre. Slightly less. Slightly not enough.

She poured herself a generous glass, drained it, then poured another before stepping back outside.

"Thanks," Andrea said, accepting the glass.

Abby didn't like the quiet that followed. She wanted desperately to break it, but wasn't about to initiate small talk with Josh's (for all intents and purposes) wife. She sipped from her glass and watched as Andrea did the same, as if she'd been dared, as if not taking a drink at that moment would mean she was weak.

It was clear she wasn't weak. She sat straight, didn't shy away from eye contact. She revelled in the silence stirring between them.

Andrea barely flinched, not feeling the need to prepare her body to speak, nor prepare for a response that would follow when she did, she just began. "It's strange," she said, "putting a face to the notion of you. I never even knew your name all these years. You floated over us like an unseen orb, hovering close sometimes, or drifting off in the distance. Always there though." She paused, studying her. "Now, here you are."

"I knew about you too," Abby admitted. "I knew you meant something to him the first time he came back.

"When he came back for *you*, you mean." Her tone was pointed. She wasn't asking for clarification; she just wanted to expand on Abby's statement.

"I sensed, at the time, that he had left someone behind and wasn't dealing with it well."

Andrea instinctively laughed. "Is that why you didn't take him back?" she asked. "Because you had a feeling he left something unresolved?"

"It was…it was more complicated than that," Abby said. "It wasn't me who contacted him, you know. It was Grace. I was getting married. I was already pregnant with A.J."

"I got pregnant with Janey right after he left," Andrea said.

"He went back to you," Abby reminded her.

"His return…came at a cost." The elusive context was stored deep in Andrea's tone.

"When it came to…Josh," Abby began, having a hard time getting his name out in front of her, "I often felt like I was the one coming up short. First, it was because of my sister. Then you. The idea of you."

Andrea chuckled. "You can't be serious."

"I am," Abby said.

Andrea leaned forward, studying the micro-expressions in Abby's face, pausing as if she thought Abby might announce she was joking at any moment. "I'm not sure if you're insane or delusional."

Abby sat further back in her chair, crossing her arms while attempting to channel any part of herself that might still contain a shred of self-assurance. "Maybe I'm neither."

"Maybe you're both," she said lightly, softening the sting of her words. "So what does that make me?" she added, inviting a sense of camaraderie between them.

"You two have been together for a long time," Abby said. "I guess that makes you loyal." She softly tacked on, "And in love."

Andrea was quick to point out, "Those are two different things. I'm not sure that I'm either."

"Why would you tell me that?"

"I don't know. I feel weirdly connected to you through him. I feel like we already know each other in some ways."

"You remind me of my sister," Abby said, a fragile vulnerability brewing beneath her ribs.

"Really?"

Abby nodded while Andrea continued to smile at what she had perceived as a compliment. Abby wasn't entirely sure she meant to flatter her with the comparison, but figured a positive reaction was just as well.

"I know how he feels about you," Andrea revealed, her face hardening with a dip in her pitch. "I've always known."

"I'm with someone, Andrea. I had to let Josh go a long time ago."

"Don't worry, I won't make you admit you still love him. I've never asked him to admit to me his feelings for you. It would be too difficult to hear it out loud from either of you. But I've seen it on his face every day for twenty years. I saw it on your face that day at Costco. I saw it again this morning." She took a sip of her drink. "I see you trying to conceal it even now."

"Maybe you're just seeing the history. A lot happened back then."

"You must think I'm crazy for staying with him. I've come here telling you I've always known he loves you, and yet I stayed." Andrea shifted in her seat, pulling her body away from the table. "Until very recently, you were a figment. You weren't something that could be grasped, something that could be sitting in front of me, drinking wine and denying what's obvious. Meeting you hasn't quelled the fears I had about my relationship, Abby, it has affirmed them tenfold."

"What is it that you want from me, then?"

Andrea hung her head, laughing helplessly and shaking away perceptible signs of embarrassment. "I honestly don't know."

"Are you going to tell him that you spoke to me? Does he know you're here now?"

"No," she answered quickly. "He's busy in his workshop. He's building something. A passion project." She took another sip of wine, holding it in her mouth for a few seconds before swallowing. "He used to get excited when he had an idea to build something new. He'd spend a whole evening describing it in detail, sketching it out at the table after dinner, telling me how much I'd love it when it was done. He hasn't said a word to me about this one." She glanced up at Abby. "I think his passion might be aimed elsewhere."

"Maybe it's a surprise," Abby guessed, remembering all of the times she'd been surprised by something Josh had built for her. The keepsake box, the crib, the rocking chair, the wooden animal toys for Alex.

"I doubt it," she said softly. "I'm not going to ask you to keep our conversation a secret. What you do about what I've told you is completely up to you."

"What if I told you that I don't intend to do anything?" Abby posed.

Andrea shrugged her shoulders. "If you want him," she said evenly, "go get him. I'm sure he'd go willingly. I'm sure he's already made that clear."

"He hasn't," Abby lied.

"Did he tell you I cheated?" she asked. "I bet he did. It was a while ago and it was with someone we both knew very well. I didn't think we'd get back together after that. In fact, it was his idea." She paused, tucking strands of hair behind her ear. "I thought for a while that it really was a clean slate. Maybe he did too. Or maybe he was just waiting for you because he knew how much it would hurt me when it was."

A hot surge of anger rushed from her stomach to the top of her head. Abby's anguish deepened the longer she sat motionless, staring at the woman who had marched into her home on a mission to disrupt her life. She grew increasingly unnerved—and far less tolerant—as she considered that this woman's daughter had behaved similarly toward her son that morning.

"I'm not going to serve as his retaliation against you," Abby stated.

"I'm sure," Andrea began, with a surprising tremor in her jaw, "that seeing you again has made him believe this is his out."

"This is between the two of you." Abby gulped a mouthful of wine. "Whatever you think I represent is likely misguided. I don't need to see Josh ever again. I won't if that's what you want, but you should sort this out with him."

"I'd never order you to stay away from him. Or him from you, for that matter," Andrea said.

"So, how do you want things to go from here?"

Andrea bit her bottom lip, hesitating before she confessed, "Part of me wants you to wake up every day knowing that I know what you are to him. The other part of me simply takes comfort in knowing that you're the only other person in the world who truly understands this mess we're caught up in."

Chapter 19: AN UNFORESEEN ALLY

She didn't go straight home. It wasn't worse than she expected. It was exactly what she'd feared. Only now it had a face. Andrea always knew she was up against a powerful force in Josh's past, but she never expected to come face to face with it like this. Never expected to have their children somehow involved. In a church parking lot, around the corner from Abby's home, Andrea pulled in to make a phone call.

"Andy?" His voice jumped, unable to hide his surprise.

"I'm sorry to call like this," she said. "I know it's been a while."

"That's okay. I'm just finishing some things up at work. Everything alright?"

"Honestly, I don't know. Can you talk for a minute?"

"Umm…yeah, sure," he said, speaking lower as though he was suddenly required to practice discretion.

"I met her," Andrea said. "She's here, Ben. In Halifax. It's so fucked up. Our kids know one another for chrissakes. She's been here for years, but he only just found out."

"What are you talking about?" he asked calmly, trying to pacify her panic.

"Josh's *one that got away*. The one he was so messed up about when he first came to Edmonton."

"That was over twenty years ago, Andy. Surely, that's all water under the bridge by now."

"I can assure you, it's not. I just left her house. It's very clear to me that she feels the same way he does. Neither one of them has fully let go of the other. It's painful to be in the same room with the two of them."

"I'm sorry," Ben sighed. "That can't be easy."

"I feel like I don't have a leg to stand on. I can't very well tell either of them to ignore their feelings for one another. Not after what you and I did."

There was a long pause on the line. Ben Hayes didn't like to be reminded of the affair. Though he stayed in touch with Andy in secret, his friendship with Josh was effectively over—for obvious reasons.

"It was his obsession with her that drove me to you in the first place."

"Our affair wasn't his fault, Andy. There were certainly better ways for you two to work out your relationship problems. I never wanted to make them worse, but I knew better."

"I know. I did too. I'm sorry for bringing it up. I don't know what to do. I can't just go home and pretend like everything's fine. He knows that I know something is up. I haven't felt this rattled since he found out about us. This is big."

"Are you sure?" Ben asked gently. "Have you talked to him at all about this?"

"No, of course not. What would I say?"

"Well, that depends," he said, "what do you want?"

Andrea glanced up, like she was looking past the encroaching ceiling of her car. She didn't quite know if she was looking to the sky or to the heavens. Was she looking for an answer she didn't have, or the strength to admit to a truth she already knew? "I don't know," she whispered hesitantly into the bottom of her cell.

"Maybe you just need to sleep on it," he suggested.

"I've been sleeping on it for twenty years, Ben."

"What about Janey?"

"She's wrapped up with this woman's son, if you can believe that," Andrea explained. "The two of them are reenacting our life right in front of us. Turns out this boy doesn't even want Jane. He's in love with someone else. Janey's convinced herself he's the one. She painted his street. That's how it all sort of blew up this morning. All of us were content in our own delusions and denial until we were forced to deal with the writing on the road."

Ben chuckled. "Jane always had a way of bringing people together." Then, with a despondent shift in his tone, as if you could hear the shameful tilt of his head on the line, he added, "And keeping them together."

"She's almost grown now, Ben. I don't think staying together for the kid makes as much sense as it did a decade ago."

Ben sighed, hints of frustration seeping through the line. Was she testing him, teasing him? Taking the temperature of his love and loyalty? It was always so hard to tell with Andrea. Her motives were never obvious. Never apparent in the top layer of her behaviour.

"At the end of the day, you chose each other," he said. "More than once. That counts for something. I think you should talk to Josh."

She laughed helplessly. She had chosen him, yes. But she was reminded now, again, that he had never fully chosen her. "He wouldn't even marry me," she said, the laugh dying halfway through. "I stopped bringing it up years ago. Has he just been waiting for her all this time?"

"Hey, I never got married," Ben pointed out, mirroring her laugh.

"Who are you waiting for?" she asked, teasing.

He didn't say anything, just let an audible puff of air travel through the phone.

She held the device to her ear, wishing she could see his face. She couldn't initiate a video call at this point in the conversation. What else was there to say? She couldn't stare at him in his shop in Edmonton. Tucked away in his office, wanting to be supportive, but knowing he was needed, or worse, wanting to be somewhere else.

She hadn't seen his face in a few years now. She had FaceTimed him during the pandemic. She'd been fighting with Josh. They were home so much together, it had become unbearable. She snuck out to Josh's workshop and made the call late one night, part of her knowing, and revelling in the fact that calling her ex-lover from Josh's sacred space was cruel. She meant it to be.

They texted every month or so. The topics were usually limited to updates about Jane, or about Andrea's work. He never inquired after Josh. She never volunteered anything about the man she chose in the end. Sometimes, she wondered if perhaps she was still somewhere in the middle. Maybe Josh wasn't the end after all. That rationale would certainly fit better right now.

"I should go," she finally said.

"Okay," he said quickly, then hesitated like there might be more.

"Thanks for listening." She had a misplaced cheeriness in her tone.

"Anytime," he offered.

Chapter 20: A DEFLATED DELUSION

It was dusk by the time she got home. She'd never told him she left. He was out back at the time. She'd been stewing in the house when she decided to go see Abby alone. Jane had texted that she was at a friend's place. The tracking app confirmed this. Josh was still home. Or, at least his cell phone was pinging from home on the app and his truck was in the driveway.

She waited in the car once the ignition was off, preparing herself to face him. Wondering if he'd look different to her now that she knew more about the things he put so much effort into keeping from her. The details and the depth of his love for this other woman. He couldn't hide as easily after today.

Andrea breezed through the front door routinely, kicking her shoes off and hanging her keys on a hook in the foyer. She was instantly struck by the sense that this environment had been staged. Call it women's intuition or a basic deduction of facts. It was eerily quiet. No ball game commentary. No lingering smells of food being cooked at any point throughout the day. No articles of clothing flung over the bannister or the sofa. No one had been doing any amount of living in this room since she left.

"You didn't mention you were going out," Josh muttered from a shadowed corner chair.

She hadn't seen him because he neglected to turn on the evening lights. This would have been deliberate because she'd been with him long enough to know that he was always eager to get the lamps turned on once the sun began to set.

"You're being a bit dramatic, aren't you?" she sneered. "Sulking in the dark."

"Where were you?" Josh asked, legs loosely crossed as he used his index finger to trace the rim of an empty tumbler.

"You know where I was," she told him.

"I wanted to see if you'd admit to it right away," he confessed.

"I'm not sure if you're trying to have a mob boss moment or what here, Josh, but if you have something to say to me, just say it."

"I don't want you going to Abigail Conrad's house again." Her name came out too carefully. He swallowed, his jaw tight.

"I thought she was Bouchard," Andrea corrected.

"Conrad was her maiden name."

"Well, she obviously didn't go back to it when she got divorced."

"That's beside the point," he said defensively.

"Hm," she acknowledged.

He stood up and strode two paces closer to her, past the velvet navy sofa, around the three-tiered nesting tables. "You had no right to go to her house. If anything else happens between the kids, I'll sort it out."

Andrea straightened her posture as he approached. His stature didn't intimidate her. She was five ten. She met his eyes, daring him to exert some sort of physical dominance over her. "I'm Jane's mother," she sneered. "I have a right to know what's going on in her life."

"I don't think your little visit to Abby was about Jane," he said, brushing past her toward the kitchen. He turned in her direction, crossing his arms from where he faced her, his back to the counter.

"You're right," she responded firmly. "It wasn't."

He glanced away from her, as if he was shocked by her willingness to be forthright. Maybe he thought she'd continue to link her pursuit of Abby to Jane and Alex. He shook his head at her admission but wasn't prepared with something to say next.

"I had to know her a little bit for myself, Josh. It seemed only fair."

"Fair," he repeated, raising his voice. "In what way is you going to harass someone from my past fair?"

"I didn't harass her. We had a conversation."

"About what?"

"Why don't you ask her?"

"I'm asking you. My partner. The woman I share my life with."

"But not your wife."

"Is that what this is about? The marriage thing again?"

"No," she answered truthfully. "Not really."

"What reason could you possibly have to sit down with Abby?"

"Don't be glib, Josh. This woman has been a part of our relationship, in one way or another, since it began. I had to know more about her."

"And did you get what you wanted?"

"I didn't want anything specific, just to satisfy my curiosity."

Josh commanded the tension to exit his inflexible frame. As he leaned away from the counter, his entire body took on a fluency that made even his face change shape. He wasn't smiling as he walked toward her, sweeping his hand along the marble granite countertop, but he was no longer filled with the same suspicious rage he greeted her with moments before.

It was strange to be so close to him like this, face to face in the shadows of their home, knowing what he now wanted, knowing *why* he wanted it now, and knowing that she was becoming increasingly desperate to provide it. Not just because it was a way out of, or around, their present quarrel, but because it was reminiscent of their past.

Abby may have been a part of his past, but Andrea was too. Domesticity often made them forget that there was a time when they raced toward fights like this, because the only way they knew how to resolve them was through carnal exploration.

They lay panting on the sofa when it was over. They didn't even fully undress. Pants were yanked down. His shirt was thrown off, hers stayed on. They were barely touching now. She glanced over at him, but he was looking away before he stood and fastened his jeans.

She hadn't even finished. There wasn't nearly enough time. He began going down on her seconds after he approached her. When she was good and wet, and moaning his name, he rose from his knees and turned her around to kiss her neck from behind, then encouraged her to bend forward. She splayed her hand against the wall, bracing as he took control of her the way she craved. The same way he had, years ago, when wanting her had been easier than loving her.

They both knew it.

Only now, she understood a little bit more about why.

PART 3: SAME MISTAKES

Chapter 21: AN ANCIENT TEXT

June 21st, 2025

Josh examined each letter on the screen of his phone like he was an epigraphist hired to decode ancient texts. He'd been staring at the message for well over a minute. Unblinking, disbelieving.

I want you. I want us. We should talk about this in person.

Surely, it was a joke. Or a test. Something designed for him to fail. If he went to her, the way every cell in his body yearned to go to her, he'd be failing Andrea. If he chose to ignore a solicitation like this—one he was sure would never come to him from Abby ever again—he could very well fail fate.

I want you. I want us. We should talk about this in person.

It was still there. Unchanged. Unapologetic. The message hadn't physically grown in size or changed in any way at all. She hadn't added anything after it, hadn't indicated that he was the unintended recipient of a message meant for someone else. The message was staring back at Josh now. Simple white text in a blue bubble. He didn't understand how something so rounded could feel so absolute.

He could write her back. Call her bluff. But he didn't want her to be bluffing. He didn't think she was waiting on the other end for a text response—or she'd probably given up waiting because the message carried a time stamp that was now two hours old.

She was daring him. How far was she willing to go? And why? After everything that had transpired tonight, after the way they parted ways.

After the fight with Andrea that began in the truck and followed them into the house, only to end by not ending at all. She went to the bedroom, and he passed out in his chair.

Waking, heart racing, cold and confused, this text message was among the least likely of things Josh thought he would see in the middle of the night.

* * *

June 20th, 2025

Over a dozen high schools in the city were celebrating prom on the same evening. Hordes of the soon-to-be graduates mustered in Public Gardens beforehand for photos.

There were sequins and suits in every direction. Josh sat on one of the benches around the perimeter of the central gazebo. Andrea was with Jane and a few of her eleventh-grade friends who were lucky enough to be asked to prom by a grade twelve guy. She proudly held her phone out in front of her like all the other moms, first centering the four girls in the frame, their corsaged hands on their popped-out hips. Then, it was time for the couples to arrange themselves. Janey leaned in close to her new boyfriend, Owen Shaw. A hockey guy, *the* hockey guy of the school. Rumoured to be signed by the Halifax Mooseheads for their upcoming season. A triumphant smile spread across Jane's face while her small hand rested atop his black lapel; her up-do pristine, her makeup flawless.

It became apparent in May that Jane was going to do anything in her power to get invited to this year's prom. Even if it meant coming between Owen and the girl he'd been seeing since January. She didn't have to go so far as to paint anyone's street this time. She operated just below the radar. A last-minute vacancy on the Prom Committee nudged her in the right direction when she found out that Owen himself was the Fundraising Chair. Jane worked closely with Owen to organize a charity hockey game with school team members and their families. Before the event had even occurred, the old girlfriend was out, Jane was in, and the search for a prom dress had commenced.

* * *

June 16th, 2025

"It's not even Janey's prom. I don't see why we both need to go," Josh complained when he was told earlier in the week to set time aside on Friday night.

"She's lucky to have been asked, Josh," Andrea told him. "Who knows what next year's going to look like for Janey. We should both be there to support her and Owen."

"The only kind of support that kid needs is a helmet," Josh chuckled. "Good thing he's an athlete. He can barely string a sentence together."

"I think they pair well with one another." Her inflection at the end gave her away.

"That's an insult to Janey," he replied.

"Well, going the intellectual route didn't exactly pay off for her, did it?"

"Alex isn't a bad kid," Josh muttered. "They weren't the right fit at this age."

"And at what age is *the right fit* for people like Alex and Janey? Our age? Older?"

"Time will tell," he said, flicking off their closet light after removing his watch and his button shirt. "I'm heading out back. Don't wait up."

Nestled in bed with the television on, she watched his silhouette in the walk-in closet as he shed the last traces of the day. Expecting him to join her, she exhaled in disappointment when he left the room. "I never do."

* * *

June 20th, 2025

You've got to be fucking joking, Josh overheard somewhere off to his left. He assumed the comment was boyish banter taking place beyond his sight line. He was beginning to feel as though he was an invisible spectator as he stared off past the flowers, past the cackling crowds. Staring at nothing really. Remembering that he too once participated in this tradition.

He could still recall Grace's blue dress. Her hair stiff and wreaking of hairspray. Were they happy that night? They pretended to be. The picture that remained on the Conrad mantle for years afterward would lead one to believe they were. Josh spent most of that evening in the shadows. In Grace's shadow. She was in her element. As a student of a different school and an eleventh grader at that, she glistened all evening like a just-shined apple—tempting every glance that came her way. They drank a lot. Rum and Coke in the limo on the way, and straight rum from his flask by the back doors each time they snuck outside to smoke.

His mouth salivated at the thought of a stiff drink. He imagined solid cubes clinking while he brought a chilled, weighted glass to his lips.

"Of all the places to run into *you* again," the same deep voice said from directly behind him. This statement felt more targeted than the last.

Josh didn't need to look up for confirmation as the man owning the coarse French accent arrogantly plunked himself on the same rickety green bench Josh occupied.

"How are you, Christopher?" Josh finally said, warily glancing over at Abby's ex-husband.

"I'm well, Joshua, and you?"

"No complaints," he answered.

"Somehow, I find that hard to believe."

Josh swept his gaze over the crowd, carefully scanning the clusters of teenagers for Jane, but he still didn't see her. They must have used up their time in the gazebo and found a floral patch to pose next to.

"Why is that?" Josh asked.

"Because you didn't get her in the end, did you?"

"Oh, for fucksakes," Josh huffed, jumping up to stand. He subtly rotated his shoulders before slipping his hands into his pockets, remaining focused on the glittering abstract movement ahead.

Christopher stood to meet him. "Didn't mean to pick at old wounds," he leaned in to say.

Josh glared at Christopher. "What *did* you mean?"

"Just having fun," he sighed.

"Somehow, I find that hard to believe," Josh mumbled.

"So, what brings you here, Joshua? These girls are a bit young for you, eh?"

Josh's hand tensed into a concealed fist in his pocket. Christopher's face hadn't gotten any less punchable with age. "My daughter is somewhere over there," he unhappily explained, pointing with his head.

"Ah yes," Christopher acknowledged. "Abby filled me in on what happened. Which one is the little vandal?"

"Watch it," Josh warned.

"I'm to understand that she painted the street, no?"

Josh declined to respond, allowing a welcomed silence to fall between them. He hadn't spotted Abby or Alex since they'd been in the park. He pretended he wasn't looking for her, wasn't interested in seeing her, but he'd been surveying people left and right as if he were inspecting a police lineup.

He hated that he was spotted first. Hated even more that it was Christopher Bouchard who saw him. Hated the most that Christopher was here in the present and not buried in the past where Josh would have preferred him to stay.

He saw her emerge from an offset crowd, she found him quickly and raised her eyebrows like they were each others' ports in their respective storms.

"This gorgeous woman appears to know you," Christopher whispered discreetly.

"That's my wife," Josh stated.

"Hmm," Christopher pondered, "Abby said you never married."

Josh redistributed his weight before replying. "We're not *married* married," he clarified.

"Oh," Christopher said cheerily, like this fact made him feel victorious. "Well then."

"It's a circus over there," Andrea announced.

Josh reached out for her, petting her shoulder, then guiding her to stand in his hold while he wrapped his arm around the small of her waist beside him.

He felt the surge of surprise shiver through her body at the gesture. He hadn't touched her like this in weeks. Hadn't laid claim to her like this in years. Christopher smiled politely at Andrea, though Josh understood the types of thoughts that men like Christopher had when they observed women like Andrea.

"Are you a parent of one of the kids from Halifax West?" Andrea asked, leaning into Josh's embrace. She was prepared to play the part with him. Loving parents. Perfect couple.

Christopher delighted in Josh's distress, adding an unnecessary pause before his answer. He glanced at Joshua briefly as if he were communicating how much it would please him to tell Josh's not-a-wife wife that he was Abigail Bouchard's real ex-husband.

"Yes," he finally confirmed, extending his hand for a shake. "I'm A.J. Bouchard's father, Christopher."

"Oh," Andrea breathed. She put the pieces together quickly.

She understood the intrinsic competition that would always exist between these two men.

And in that understanding, something else clicked into place.

Chapter 22: A PROPER MEAL

June 20th, 2025

When Abby located Christopher engaged in conversation with Andrea and Josh at the park, her instinct was to get him away from them.

"We should be going, Chris," she said low near his ear. "You'll want to get back to Rachel at the hotel."

"My wife's not been feeling well since we arrived. Food poisoning or something," he explained to the group.

Andrea tilted her head politely.

Josh and Abby had made brief eye contact, both extending a hint of a smile toward the other.

Looking down at Abby, and deliberately louder, Christopher said, "I'm in no rush to be stuck in a hotel room all night with someone who can't stop vomiting."

"Charming," Josh whispered under his breath.

Both women heard.

"Let's grab some dinner. You two should join us," Christopher proposed.

"I'm sure everyone has better things to do," Abby said softly.

"Nonsense. The kids will be out all night. They're chaperoned. We should be taking advantage of the freedom."

"I am starving," Andrea confessed. "I've been so busy making sure Janey's hair and makeup were just right that I haven't even eaten today."

"Joshua, are you going to let your wife starve?" Christopher condescended, his eyes gleaming with slyness as the sun dipped in the sky behind them.

"We can grab something quick on the way home," he quietly suggested.

"It would be nice to have a proper meal," Andrea said. "One that I don't have to cook."

"I'll cook for you," Josh offered.

"C'mon, come for dinner, guys," Christopher insisted.

"You're being obnoxious," Abby whispered to her ex-husband.

"You're probably just hangry, darling," he said. "Let's meet at the Italian place down on Bishop's Landing. Ristorante a Mano. Sound good?"

"I love that place," Andrea pleaded with Josh, squeezing his shoulder for emphasis."

"Okay," he mumbled.

"Wonderful," Christopher announced. "Just like old times."

Abby smiled respectfully and turned to walk with Christopher. She heard Andrea whisper to Josh behind them, *Why is it just like old times?* She didn't hear him give an answer.

"Why are you trying to start trouble?" Abby asked Christopher as he drove her car to the restaurant.

"I'm not," he lied. "I really am hungry. I'm no good to Rachel back at the hotel. She doesn't even want to smell food right now. My son is obviously busy tonight. Dinner with my ex-wife and her ex-lover seemed like the next best thing."

"Ugh, I knew I should have never told you what happened with the kids," she said, frustrated.

"You didn't. A.J. did," he corrected.

"Still," she said. "I knew you'd have a field day with it."

"Catching Joshua off guard probably will be one of the highlights of the trip," he agreed.

She shot him a scolding glare.

"Aside from our son's high school graduation, of course," he corrected.

"Can you promise me that you'll behave yourself at dinner, please? I haven't even seen him since the whole debacle with the kids. I'd prefer to keep my distance from him. I'm sure Andrea would prefer that too."

"Maybe I'll ask her if she wants to join my club."

"What are you talking about?"

"The 'I Survived Josh and Abby' club."

"You're disgusting."

"C'mon Abs. If we can't laugh about it, what else do we have? We lived to tell the tale. Got a pretty good kid out of the whole thing too. It wasn't all a bust."

"I never thought our marriage was a bust."

"I should have done things differently," he confessed.

"You think?" Abby quipped, unsure of whether she should trust his sudden vulnerability.

"Maybe I would have if there was a time during any of it that you belonged to me instead of him."

"We've been over this, Christopher," she said, sighing at the thought of entering into this conversation once again. "It won't change anything."

"Why can't you just admit it?" he asked, though the urgency with which he demanded an answer had certainly been downgraded since the last time they spoke about the impact Josh had on their marriage. "Even now. The two of you are still pretending you're not constantly fighting against some force that pulls you toward one another."

"I'm not fighting against anything. He's part of my past. It's complicated, I'll give you that. I'm still processing the fact that A.J. and Jane had some sort of relationship. We're grown now and we're not going to get anywhere dwelling on things that happened a long time ago. I've moved on."

"Why'd you break up with Ethan?"

"He's bicoastal. He wanted me to drop everything each time he was in town. It was easier to balance work and my relationship with him when he was my primary client. I could see it getting more difficult once his house was finished. I have other work I need to focus on."

"It didn't have anything to do with Joshua coming back into your life?"

"No. It was purely a coincidence that he just happened to work on Ethan's house as well."

"I don't think it was a coincidence, Abby."

"The whole thing was a weird blip. Ethan's house is done, the relationship I had with him is done, and the kids have seemingly distanced themselves from one another. I'll be fine."

"I do care about you, you know. I want the best for you."

Abby laughed. "Since when?"

"Since always. Well, probably more so since meeting Rachel," he said. "She's made me grow up. She made it pretty clear from the beginning that she wasn't into playing games. Doesn't tolerate any of the shit I used to do. I'm a changed man."

"Glad to hear it," Abby said sincerely. "Alex has always spoken highly of her. He has said you're different too. I just didn't believe him."

"It's true. It's all because of her."

"She's a better woman than I."

Christopher glanced over at Abby as they crept to a stop at a red light. “We were young, Abby. And I was too stupid to handle things maturely.”

“I suppose I was too.”

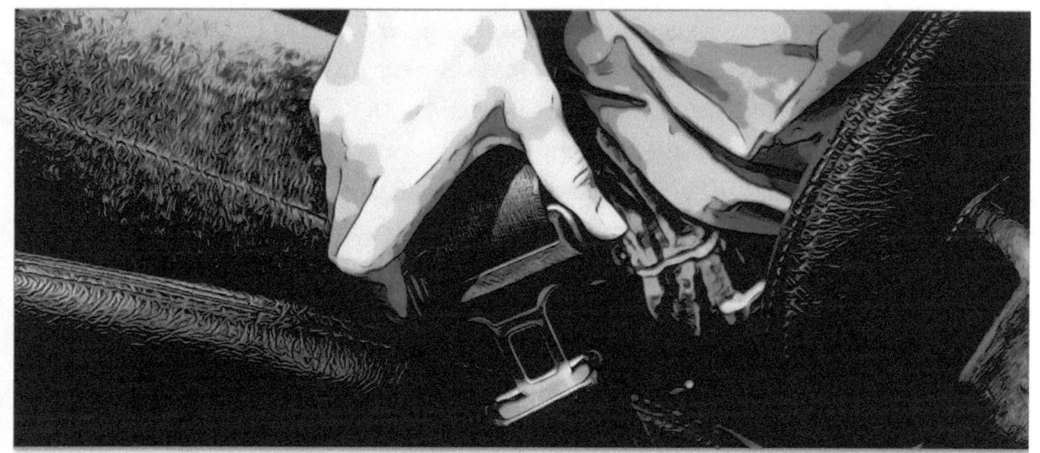

Chapter 23: A COGNITIVE DECLINE

June 21st, 2025

Abby had been lying on the couch for a while, slipping in and out of consciousness. Someone placed her living room sofa on a spinning platform. A new design feature perhaps. But she knew that couldn't be true.

It was probably the martinis. Four of them at dinner. Two was enough to dull the tension in her chest that spawned when the four of them were sat at a table together. Christopher beside her. Josh across from her. Andrea beside him. Low lights. Low ceilings. The din of a Friday night crowd buzzing around and through them. Just visible over Josh's shoulder from her spot in the booth, the slow passing of people along the waterfront outside.

She ordered a third drink out of fear that her anxiety would return before the evening was over. She ordered a fourth because she was properly drunk midway through the third.

Josh had stared conspicuously, assessing her with his loud silent judgment each time he spied signs that sobriety was escaping her. *You're half the reason this drink is necessary*, she'd thought with every gulp from the wide glass rim.

The other half, of course, being Christopher. Him taking pleasure in the misery of his dinner companions, knowing he could go back to his wife at any time, sick as she may have been. The very woman who made him *a changed man.* How changed could he really be if he still revelled in Abby's emotional distress? He was technically free of this quandary. Nothing more than an outsider looking in at this point. No doubt relieved that it was no longer his reality.

Andrea fit somewhere in there too. The two women barely exchanged a direct word all evening. They'd said plenty indirectly, through seemingly nonchalant glances and conversation additives that had intentions far beyond a casual contribution to the topic at hand.

Another dry martini, please, and keep them coming.

In bits and pieces on a non-linear timeline, Abby remembered Christopher dropping her off. He took off her shoes. She didn't want to go upstairs. Didn't want him in her bedroom. It pleased him, her vulnerability. The degradation of her composure. He made joke after joke. But he was rather gentle in the end. And that was a nice change to see in a changed man. She wondered, somewhere in her alcohol-induced cognitive decline, if he'd finally forgiven her. This retrospective lightness he exuded toward her felt like it could be forgiveness.

* * *

June 20th, 2025

He didn't like that she was leaning on Christopher to help keep herself upright. She'd never hold onto his arm the way she was now if she were sober. Even when they were married, she didn't hang off of him.

Josh and Andrea walked next to one another a few paces behind, nearly brushing arms, but not quite close enough to touch. When Josh noticed Christopher leading Abby to her car in the parking lot, he took a long stride to get to them.

"She can't drive," Josh insisted.

"Relax, Joshua," Christopher commanded. "I'll take her home and Uber back to the hotel."

"I'm fine," Abby lightly protested while trying a weak reach at Christopher for her keys.

"No!" both men said urgently in unison.

"I'll be in the truck," Andrea interrupted. "Nice to meet you, Christopher," she called out. "Goodnight, Abby."

"Bye," Abby yelled, waving her fingers. An insincere smile glazed her face.

"Lovely to meet you, Andrea," Christopher responded with extra emphasis. "Enjoy your summer. And I mean it, if you two are ever out my way, please get in touch." He caught Josh's eye.

"We don't have plans to be in Victoria anytime soon, Christopher," Josh grumbled, "but thanks."

Andrea had waltzed off. She remained pleasant all evening. Friendly even. She'd already be in the process of unravelling all of the pent-up anger she so dutifully concealed through dinner. He'd feel it when he got into the truck. Hear about it when they got home, if not sooner.

And it wasn't as if there was no case to be made. The evidence churned amongst them. In the park, at the restaurant, even now. The undeniable attraction, connection, the soul bond that dominated any space Josh and Abby occupied together.

"Pity Ethan's out of the picture," Christopher said to Abby while he directed her into the car. "He missed quite a night."

Josh remained standing near the car door, stretching his arm out to insist it be left open once Christopher had placed her inside. He crouched over close to Abby, shoving his head into the interior of the car and reaching over her with the seatbelt. "You broke up with Ethan?" he asked.

"Mm hmm," she admitted.

"Are you okay, Abby? Are you sure you're alright with…this?" he stammered, not specifying which *this* was in question.

"You're not in a position to save me anymore," she whispered. Her eyes scanned the parking lot in the direction of his truck. She pictured an impatient Andrea spying this encounter, aggrieved by their closeness. "You never really were."

Still inches from her face once the belt clicked into the slot, he made sure to wait for her eyes, locking in on them to anchor to a part of her unaffected by the booze, but perhaps intoxicated by possibility.

"Do you want to be saved?" he asked.

Christopher was seconds from opening the driver door when Abby uttered, "I want you to…"

"You want me to what?" Josh pleaded.

She heard the pull of the handle and muttered, "I want you to want me again."

Josh rapidly confessed, "I never stopped," before they were interrupted.

Christopher promptly sat himself in the car and looked over at Josh, whose head still lingered in the cabin. The sarcasm arrived on his face before he said, "You coming with us, big man?"

"No," Josh answered.

"Au revoir," Christopher yelled with a dismissive wave.

Josh glanced down one last time at Abby, who appeared to have moved on to an altogether different and distant train of thought. He quickly closed the car door and was left standing maladroit on the cracked cement of the parking lot, contemplating the rest of his life while she slipped further into the night.

* * *

June 20th, 2025

"I can't compete with history, Josh," she announced ten voiceless minutes into their long drive home.

"What are you talking about?" he grunted.

"Can we please just get this over with?"

"Are you saying you want to fight?" He asked. "Because, honestly, I'm tired and not in the mood."

She shifted her position in the passenger side, inching slightly more toward him, but still delivering her message to the windshield. "I'm tired too. I'm tired of all of it."

"Great. Let's save it for tomorrow," he said, taking one hand off the wheel to run his fingers through his dark hair.

"How are we supposed to keep going?"

"I'm going to steer this truck towards our house and eventually, we'll arrive there."

"For fucksakes, Josh. What do you want me to do?" she yelled as an uncomfortable heat rose through her torso, finally settling in her chest."Do you want me to scream? Do you want me to spell it out? Stop pretending you have no idea what I'm talking about. Don't act like you weren't sitting at that table tonight across from the love of your life while I was right beside you."

Josh guided a finger upward on the side console, opening his window a few inches to take in a slow breath of fast-moving outside air. With a stiff jaw, he quietly replied, "What do you want me to say, Andrea?"

"Something! Anything! I might as well be pleading with a goddamn wall."

"You wanted to go to dinner with them," he mumbled. "I didn't want to go."

"You're right," she admitted. "I guess, in a way, I was asking for it. Maybe I just wanted to be sure."

"Sure about what?"

She watched helplessly as faint tree line shadows swooshed by in the dusk while they drove further outside the city limits toward the home they shared. "That we could survive this," she sighed, continuing to stare out her window and away from him. "Now, after tonight, I can see that we won't."

Chapter 24: AN INCONVENIENT FAVOUR

June 20th, 2025

Christopher navigated the streets of Halifax like he was a stunt driver. He weaved through backroads, veering from the normal route to Clayton Park each time the car was forced to stop for more than a few seconds. The Friday night traffic became less congested as he exited the downtown core.

"I forgot how terrible of a driver you are," Abby said.

"I'm in a bit of a rush to get back to my wife," he stated, as if he were executing an inconvenient favour.

"Nobody asked you to hijack my car and take me home."

"We both know you're in no condition to drive," he bluntly reminded her. "Perhaps you were hoping that if you got too out of sorts, someone else was going to swoop in and rescue you."

"Shut up, Christopher," Abby hissed.

"I've never seen you perform for him the way you did tonight. Or maybe I was just blind to it back then."

"I wasn't *performing* for anyone. I was obviously uncomfortable being at dinner with all of you and I had too much to drink. Fucking sue me."

"Don't be saucy. It never suited you."

"Don't tell me what to do," she quipped back. "I never listened."

"The only thing you didn't listen to was your vows."

Abby hurled a shocked bundle of hot air from her mouth. "You're one to talk, you hypocrite."

"I wouldn't have been looking for anyone else if I'd been happy at home."

"You're such a liar," she said. "Age has made you forgetful."

Christopher switched to playful when he said, "I haven't forgotten a thing. Still sharp as a whip."

Abby didn't loosen her fury to match him. Still tense and unrelenting, she confessed, "I never would have married you if I hadn't gotten pregnant with A.J."

"No need to remind me, Abby. You spent the entirety of our marriage letting me know that I was never your first choice."

She glanced out the window unresponsive because he was right. Maybe she was too young at the time to articulate it, but every ounce of energy she gave to Christopher back then was chained to the resentment she felt toward him for being the reason she wasn't with Josh.

"If we hadn't gotten pregnant, do you think you'd be with him now?"

Flipping her head back toward Christopher, she blurted, "Who?"

"Don't be naive," he scolded.

"Don't tell me what to do," she repeated, quietly adding, "I don't know. He was with Andrea then. He's with her now. They seem happy. I don't want to get in the way."

"They're not happy," Christopher stated.

"How do you know?"

"I've got a keen sense of awareness about these things after being married to you," he joked.

"I could have benefitted from something like that when I was married to *you*," she replied.

"Anyway, you can see it. They're not happy. He can't keep his eyes off you. Probably can't keep his thoughts off you either. Andrea doesn't appear to be a stupid woman. And I think it's safe to say you've already gotten in the way. Whether you meant to or not."

"Settle down, Dr. Phil," Abby chided. "None of us are seeking relationship advice from *you*."

"Maybe you ought to. I'm the only one who's happily married."

"And yet, here you are on a Friday night, squabbling with your ex-wife."

"Rebecca's sick. I'm heading straight back to her after I drop you off."

"Heaven forbid you spend an evening taking care of someone when there's nothing in it for you."

Christopher took a full breath in and let it out again. "I'm taking care of *you* right now, aren't I?"

"You probably thought there would be something in it for you," Abby said.

"You mean *besides* the absolute pleasure of your company?"

"Hmph," she huffed.

"Maybe I just wanted to make sure my son still had a mother in the morning, eh? Stop playing games with me, Abs. Stop playing games with yourself. And for the love of god, stop playing games with Joshua and his wife, or whatever the hell she is. If you two want each other as badly as all the eye fucking would suggest, stop hurting other people. Let all that shit from the past go." He paused, staring straight into the dark suburban street ahead. "Live your life, Abby," he told her. "Stop running from it."

Chapter 25: AN OVERWHELMING WANT

June 20th, 2025

The cool June air funnelled eagerly through her lungs, pushing down the stale gin teasing a resurgence.

"Don't touch me," she barked, feeling the light pressure of his fingertips on her waist.

"Just guiding the way," Christopher replied under his breath.

He stood back, impatiently observing her digging for her keys in her purse, then fumbling to get the correct one into the lock.

"I can take it from here," she told him. "Thanks for the drive. I'll see you and Rachel for dinner on Sunday."

"Can I at least wait in the house while I order an Uber?"

"Fine," she agreed.

Abby strung her bag on the banister and proceeded into the living room. She felt worse now that she was home. The dizziness was far more unbearable sitting still on the sofa than it had been while they were driving. She didn't want to be weak in front of Christopher. She'd had just about enough of his superiority complex.

"Uber should be here in ten," he announced behind her. "Why don't you let me get you settled upstairs in your room?"

"I don't think so," she said.

"I'm serious. You should get some sleep. You're going to feel like trash in the morning."

"I feel like trash right now," she told him.

"All the more reason to get to bed," he said.

"You're not getting anywhere near my bedroom, Christopher."

"Don't flatter yourself," he said.

"You've never been one to turn down an indecent proposal," she teased, fighting a battle against her own narrowing eyes and losing.

Waltzing further into the living room to face her, his hands smugly in his pockets, he bent slightly to say, "Are you making one?"

"You wish," she bellowed.

Christopher shook his head and strode out of her sightline to the kitchen. She faintly heard the clinking of glass and the splashing sounds of the running faucet.

"You know," he began, the sound of his voice growing closer as he approached her once again, "your flirtations, while charming and nearly impossible to resist, are misdirected."

"I'm not…" she started, but was cut short by Christopher's finger on her mouth.

"Shhhh," he insisted. "Take these, drink this, use this if you need anything." Christopher placed Advil capsules and a glass of water on the table next to her cell phone.

Once his touch was on her skin, it was as if she was under a spell. The familiar feeling of his warmth on her, the same pressure, same sensation that she never really loved, but once upon a time liked because it made her feel wanted. She hated wanting him now. Hated enjoying that he had gently shifted her body, placing her head on a couch pillow, before moving to remove her shoes.

She wondered if he'd kiss her first. She was ashamed to admit that she wanted him to. She was still drunk enough that she could imagine it was Josh and that thought was comforting to her. He stood up, she presumed to remove some or all of his clothing, but reached for a throw blanket first. He spread out the blanket as she lay willful and waiting, though a bit confused as to why a blanket was necessary at this moment.

He spread the blanket over her, tucking her feet underneath, and whispered, "Goodnight Abby. Get some rest."

It was as if reality had reappeared with the closing of the door behind Christopher. Abby shook off a shiver that ran through the entire length of her body. She prayed that her perception of what had just happened was worse than the way the actual events unfolded.

How drunk had she been to convince herself that sleeping with her re-married ex-husband was a good idea? Not even a good idea, an idea at all! It should never have presented in her mind as an option. Why did she toy with the concept, teasing him, seducing him like some old lush in the corner of a bar?

What would Josh think of her if she'd gone through with it? Knowing Christopher, he'd find some way to disclose it to him, though she wasn't sure if or when she'd ever see Josh again. She recalled his reach across her chest. Him securing her seatbelt, their faces so close she could have leaned ever so slightly to place her lips on him. Christopher was right; everything Abby had said and done since leaving the restaurant was misdirected. He told her to use her phone if she needed anything. Alone in an empty house, while desire coursed through her, and inhibitions were clearly scarce, she didn't need for anything—but the want, the want was unrestrained.

She reached for her phone on the table and scrolled to his name in her contacts. She wanted to write the words, not send them. She wanted to own her feelings. See them there on the screen attached to his name. Something about that felt powerful. After she typed it, the empowerment increased. The desire grew. She was feeling brave enough to decide that tomorrow she'd have to address these feelings. Or perhaps on Monday, after A.J.'s graduation.

Not tonight.

Not over text.

Not like this.

But soon, a real conversation could and should be had. She loved Josh. She wanted him. And she was fairly certain he felt the same way. There was a lot of other factors that had to be considered, but there was more risk evolving as the root of the issue continued to be ignored. Scared as she was to stop running, she knew they'd been put in each other's paths again so they could find a way to stand still.

Her eyelids fell heavy, uncontrollably dense and determined to close, so she glanced at the screen through the small slit of sight that remained before surrendering to sleep, hoping the same level of resolve would still be present when she woke.

Her thumb drifted.

Her eyes closed.

Her body let go.

And when the screen darkened, the message had been sent.

Chapter 26: A CHANGED MAN

June 20th, 2025

To his surprise, Rachel was coming out of the bathroom, dressed and moving spritelier than before, when he quietly inched his way into the hotel room. The air was stale but not quite as oppressive as when he left. Some of her things that were on the floor had been tidied. She wore purple athletic leggings and a black sports bra now as she walked toward the bed, smiling when she noticed that he had returned.

"How was it?" she asked. "I'm sure A.J looked very handsome."

"Obviously," Christopher replied. He leaned over to kiss the side of her face when they met at the foot of the bed. "How are you feeling, my love? You look much better."

"I think I'm finally coming out of it," she told him. "I got a shower, brushed my teeth."

"In that case," he said, moving in to kiss her longer this time on the lips.

"I'm not feeling *that* good," she said teasingly as she pulled away.

"Worth a shot," he said, stroking the ends of damp blonde hair draped over her shoulder.

"How's Abby?" Rachel asked cheerily.

"She's…" he began, trying to summon the right words in English to describe someone he perceived to be a beautiful disaster. "She's good. We went to dinner after the photos."

"Just the two of you?" Rachel asked, attempting to mask her alarm.

"No, with another couple. Remember, I told you what A.J. told me about the girl with the paint? Well, it was that girl's parents. The father is someone Abby's sister dated in high school."

"*Another* couple," Rachel bluntly repeated. "You and Abby aren't a couple anymore."

"I know, babe, but you know what I mean."

"So there were four of you at dinner and the other man was someone who dated A.J.'s aunt who passed away?"

He took off his watch at the small table by the window and began to unbutton his shirt. "Pretty much."

Christopher peered over at his wife, lying on the bed, looking healthier than before. Her legs were crossed casually at the ankle, her back propped up on flattened pillows that she'd been clutching for most of the day.

He thought of the way he left Abby. Drunk and desperate on her sofa, knowing he could have taken from her what she hated giving him all those years ago. Tonight, she had practically thrown it at him, and he very intentionally dropped the ball.

"That sounds…complicated," Rachel observed, splitting her attention to include the Netflix menu.

"It's tragic," he added, plopping down on the bed beside her and casually assessing the recommended options on screen. "None of these people have grown up. Except for A.J."

"Maybe they're all feeling a bit nostalgic," she suggested. "It being prom season and all."

"Maybe," he voiced noncommittally. "I think they're all still full of shit."

Rachel chuckled under her breath and nuzzled in closer to him after selecting an episode of the newest Harlen Coben series. "That's not your life anymore, Chris," she whispered.

"Thank god," he muttered.

Chapter 27: AN INAPPROPRIATE WAGER

June 21st, 2025

The porch lights were off when he pulled into the driveway behind her car, but he could see that a lamp was on in the living room. He tried the front door, testing the lock, hating to feel it click open under his grasp. She'd been here for hours. Alone, unstable, and unprotected.

"Abby!" he yelled before spotting her sprawled out asleep on the sofa.

She stirred at the noise but slipped back into a dream state.

He kneeled in front of her, stopping to assess what he saw. Shoes off, a blanket placed over her. A glass of water and some ibuprofen waiting on the coffee table for when she was alert enough to know that she needed them. Christopher had done this. He'd taken care of her.

Josh's chest went tight, pinching his breath as he wondered if that was all her ex-husband did before he left.

Her phone was there on the table next to the glass. He touched the screen for reasons he didn't want to acknowledge before giving himself permission to do it. There were no notifications, just a photograph that looked to be a couple of years old. Alex, looking back at the camera, the beach behind him, numbers that read 2:17 hovering above his head.

He thought about leaving. He knew she was alright as he stared at the small rise and fall of her chest while she slept. He could pretend he never came here in the middle of the night. That he hadn't made the incredibly rash and unwise decision to acquiesce to the command of a woman who'd had too much to drink at dinner.

Maybe he could get back to the house before Andrea knew he was gone. Maybe he could redirect the energy he'd been investing in Abby since seeing her last month, or even better, since seeing her twenty-three years ago. He could forget about Abby for good and focus on the woman who was asleep next to the outline of his body that had developed over time in their bed.

Being here now could change the rest of his life. But he wasn't concentrating on that, not entirely. All he wanted was to share a few moments with her in the still of the night, without the rest of their respective lives getting in the way, and without the ghosts from their respective pasts reminding them of all the reasons that the past is best left behind them.

"Abby," he whispered near her face. "Abby, it's me."

She stirred again, as though acknowledging him from behind her closed eyes.

He touched her face, the warmth of her cheek sending a bolt of excitement up his arm. She leaned into his touch, lightly smiling. He couldn't tell if she knew it was him, or if the motion of his palm on her skin was playing an alternate role in her dream. He grazed the smoothness near her mouth with his thumb before moving it further to softly trace the outline of her parted lips.

Her eyes opened slowly, happily seeing him before she could register that he was there. The realization, when it arrived seconds later, caused her to jolt her body back.

"Jesus, what are you doing here?" she groaned.

"You said you wanted to talk. You said you wanted me," he answered.

She sat up unsteadily, adjusting her shirt when she noticed it was hanging low to reveal her bra. "I shouldn't have done that. I didn't mean it," she whispered.

Josh got up from a crouching position to place himself on the sofa beside her. "So, should I turn around and go?"

"What time is it?" she asked groggily.

"It's after two," he answered, staring down at his hands in his lap.

"Where does Andrea think you are?"

"I don't know. I don't think she cares much. We had a fight."

"About what?" she snapped, glancing over at him.

He turned his head to face her. "She thinks there's something going on between us."

"Is there?" Abby said.

"You messaged me, Abby." He stood up as the steady flush rushing to his face became too unnerving to neglect. "I knew that this stupid dinner was going to be a bad idea. I knew it would force something neither one of us was prepared to deal with. I can't believe I didn't fight harder against it."

Ignoring what he'd said about the message, Abby jumped right into her default defensive mode. "You wanted the opportunity to puff your chest just as much as Christopher did," she stated.

"Oh please," Josh hissed, "I'm nothing like him."

"He's not quite as insufferable as he used to be," she said.

"He seemed the exact same to me," Josh muttered.

She shrugged her shoulders.

"Do you have some newfound admiration for the guy?" Josh asked, summoning the same indignant tone he used to reserve for conversations about Christopher Bouchard.

"He was decent enough to get me home and make sure I was okay," she explained, remembering only pieces from earlier in the night. "It's taken years for him and I to get to this place. We're finally able to be civil with one another."

"Do you hear yourself? You're waxing poetic about your *ex*-husband, Abby. You left the guy for a reason."

"I left him for a million reasons."

"My point exactly," he said. "All of that is forgotten because he got you home without incident?" Josh asked. "Please tell me there weren't any incidents."

There wasn't a clear enough picture in her mind of what had happened between the restaurant and now, and Abby was too embarrassed to admit that she'd lost time as a consequence of just trying to loosen tension tonight. "Did you come here to grill me about Christopher?" she asked.

"No," he replied. "I came here because you told me to."

"Nothing happened with Christopher," Abby said with almost certainty. "Except that for a few minutes, I didn't completely detest him. But I can assure you nothing happened. I wouldn't even let him take me to my bedroom."

"Why did you send me that message?" he asked her, perching down on the arm at the opposite end of her sofa.

Abby took a moment before answering, unsure of what message he was referring to. Had she said something directly to him earlier, something that weighed on his mind to such a degree that he drove to her house in the middle of the night? Was it something more discreet, or subliminal?

In an effort to buy herself some time, and because he was already mad at Andrea, Abby conveniently recalled a token from their conversation in the backyard last month. "Andrea told me that if I expressed any sort of interest in you, you would probably show interest back. She said you'd 'go willingly'."

"Are you kidding me?" he scoffed, rising to his feet once again. "Who says that shit?"

"Josh, you're here, aren't you?"

"Are you two co-conspirators now? What the hell, Abby?"

"I'm sorry," she admitted. She held her head in her hands, pressing tight on the sides like she could pressure cook her thoughts to completion with a bit of applied force. All she could summon at that point were visions from across the table at dinner, the very thing that made her drown her short-term memory in gin.

"I watched you with her this evening. I saw the looks that you gave one another. The quiet language you share. You've raised a child together. It was like watching you with Grace, only worse because I'm not missing out on some teenage-imagined idea of being with you like I was back then. I was reminded tonight of just how much I gave up all those times that I convinced myself not to love you."

"So what are you saying? You want me to blow up my life because you made an inappropriate wager with my girlfriend and then got a drunken case of FOMO?"

"No," she insisted, shooting up from the couch. "I don't want you to do anything."

Josh pulled his cell phone from his pocket, dramatically retrieving the message she'd sent. He walked closer, holding the screen out toward her. "Three hours ago you wanted me," he said. "In person."

She saw the message first, then an urgent recollection of the night's events cascaded into her memory. Her pathetic moment with Christoper, her resolve to talk to Josh. Her typing the message and deciding not to send it. And now, the realization that it no longer mattered if she sent it by accident or on purpose. She was humiliated either way.

"I'm sorry," Abby said, gravitating slowly toward the kitchen and placing a firm hand on the island counter for support.

Josh walked a few paces, setting his weight against the back edge of the sofa to face her. "I'm here now," he said, voice low. "The question is, what are you gonna do with me?"

Chapter 28: A HAPLESS ULTIMATUM

June 21st, 2025

Abby's mouth curled up, shaking her head as an exasperated wind raced past her lips. "You arrogant son of a bitch."

"I won't do this," he said, shaking his head back and forth.

"Do what?" she taunted.

"I won't fight with you until we're both so wound up that we have angry sex, just so you can regret it afterwards."

"Good," she huffed. "I wasn't planning on having any kind of sex with you." Though she shuddered at the thought.

"I doubt that's what you were thinking when you hit send on that message," he said.

"So what do we do?" she asked him. "We've ruled out the only two things we're any good at together."

Reminding her of a comment she made to him years ago, he said, "Fighting and fucking."

"Precisely," she agreed.

They stared at one another, simmering in the discomfort of their hapless ultimatum. The house remained eerily silent around them. The lights warm and dim and familiar. The ultimatum itself all too familiar. Josh hadn't felt the need to remind her of their brief exchange before Christopher brought her home. Was it worth reliving the dialogue that really brought them to this? The true origin of tonight's temptation. Miscommunication? A liquor-fuelled Freudian slip? Maybe. Maybe not.

"I should go," he eventually said. He wasn't sure if he was baiting her, or if sheer exhaustion had ultimately won.

He wasn't sure he could do this again. If this was it, he'd go home and he'd tell Andrea that he was done with Abby. And he'd mean it. He'd tell Andrea he was done wanting Abby, done mourning the many losses of her. Done resenting Andrea for not being her.

There was a discerning part of him that believed it could be true this time. He didn't know if Andrea would accept it and willingly return to the same arrangement they'd had now for well over a decade. If she was aware that he'd left the house, maybe the damage was already done.

"Okay," she agreed. Just like that. No rush to counter. No panic at the thought of his absence. No signs of her comprehending his determination to depart from her for good.

He could feel his intention to go. He sensed it pulling him toward the door. He could visualize opening the door, then closing it behind him, into the night and an unknown future. Maybe he'd glance back at the house before he got in the truck, nostalgic, but still resolved to leave her where she stood.

His legs hadn't moved.

His feet were still fixed to the floor.

"Or, you could stay," she said quietly.

His eyes shot up from the floor. He thought he'd misheard her. "What?"

"Stay. Josh," she repeated.

"Okay," he breathed.

She brought her hands up in front of her, clasping them and fidgeting with her fingers as she spoke. "I don't want to blow up your life. I think I already have. I didn't know you were here in the city. I swear. Now that you're here in my house, I'm telling you I don't want you to go. I don't know what that means. I don't know what happens next. I just know I don't want you to go. I want you…" Her shoulders fell as she exhaled. She whispered once more, "I want you."

Chapter 29: A POTENTIAL PRICE

He walked to her slowly, afraid he might fracture the moment if his steps were too quick or too sharp.

"You want me," he echoed, checking her eyes for confirmation.

She looked up at him, nodding slowly.

His lips curled on one side. "How do you want me, Abby?"

"We shouldn't do anything tonight," she decided, glancing away from him.

"I won't touch you until you tell me to," he whispered so close to her face she was breathing in his exhale.

"Stay here with me," she urged. "Just to sleep. Sleep beside me. That's all I want right now."

He stood unwavering before her. "You won't even let me kiss you?"

"No," she answered. "Not until we figure things out. If we're gonna do this…and I'm not necessarily saying that we are… ultimately it's your decision… and I think you need to take some real time to make it…but *if* we were to do this, we can't make the same mistakes we made before."

"What do you mean, IF, Abby? Josh countered. "I'm in this, I'm here, aren't I?"

"It's the middle of the night, Josh. I drank a lot at dinner and you had a fight with Andrea. Those aren't the right circumstances for making life-altering decisions."

He swayed backward, shifting his weight as he put space between them. "Our circumstances have always been impossible. They won't be any easier tomorrow, or the next day, or the day after that."

"You're right," she said, "they could be much more difficult in the morning. You might wake up and realize that you don't want to turn your back on everything you've built with her for me."

"For *us*, Abby," he corrected. "Don't do this. Don't do the second-guessing thing now. Don't tell me you want me and then follow it with all the reasons why we shouldn't be together." He stepped forward again, reaching for her arm at her side. He sandwiched her cold hand between both of his and went on, "I know you don't know how to want me in a way that isn't at a cost. This time the cost is mine. You said it yourself, it's my decision. But do you really think this is a question for me?"

"The kids," Abby said as if it had only just occurred to her. "We'd have to be very careful about how we approach this with the kids."

"Janey is stubborn, but she'll come around," Josh supposed. "I'm sure Alex just wants his mother to be happy."

"I'm sure Jane wants the same for her mother," Abby said. "She'll think I'm the home-wrecking mom of the boy who broke her heart."

"Let me deal with Jane," Josh said.

"I'm scared, Josh," Abby confessed. "I still don't have the courage to… claim you for myself."

Josh placed her hand on his cheek. He took hold of her other hand, setting it on his opposite cheek, then fixed an impassioned gaze past her eyes and into a part of her that few people who knew her could see. "I'm already yours, Abby."

The only thing left to do was to seal their intention with a kiss. A powerful kiss. An earnest, long-awaited, future-affirming, kiss.

The gaze continued, but the kiss never came.

Her fingers slipped from his face and she trailed his arm until she could lightly grasp his hand with hers. Silently, she led them to the sofa where she gently encouraged him to sit first so she could curl in close beside him.

He wrapped his arm around her and pulled a blanket over their legs. Within minutes, her breathing settled into a steady rhythm against his chest. He tightened his hold on her, resisting the urge to chase what the morning might bring.

For now, he let the quiet stand.

Chapter 30: AN ABRUPT DISCLOSURE

June 20th, 2025

Twinkle lights flickered in the middle of a round table draped in white linen. Overdressed teenagers in suits and gowns played at being old-world adults, chatting over synthesized music now lowered for the meal.

They'd danced and mingled and laughed through the 'most likely' awards. They were served apple-glazed pork medallions and whipped garlic potatoes before the chocolate lava cakes topped with vanilla ice cream.

Janey sat next to Owen at a table they shared with some of his teammates and their girlfriends. She extended her charm to the friends of his who supported their conveniently-timed union, sticking her nose up at those who did not. Her reputation had taken a notable hit after the incident with Alex. The whole episode had been coined Paint Jane.

But then she got in front of the joke, claiming #paintjane on socials and posting a video at least once a week of herself lip-syncing lyrics to scorned lover indie-pop songs. When she did the bridge to Gracie Abrams' *That's So True*, Jane got nearly fifteen-thousand views.

Two tables away, behind Jane and Owen, A.J. and Sarah were sitting close to one another. He held her hand in his lap. Neither could seem to blend in, feeling restricted in their formal dress, and keenly aware of their elevated status as one of the top school couples that other students kept tabs on. It was vastly different this time around. They'd been ranked much lower when they dated in the tenth grade.

By eleventh grade, they'd been included as a blip on the high school couples map once word got out that they began sleeping together. A.J. selfishly started to pull away from Sarah when he noticed that his status as a sexually active member of the student body had become a topic of conversation amongst people he barely knew.

This relationship shift coincided with physical changes in A.J. He'd entered high school at nearly six feet tall and crossed the threshold entirely during the summer between tenth and eleventh grade. His shoulders got wider, his muscles grew more defined with the help of his summer roofing job, and his sparse facial hair had evened out.

Other girls' perception of him had changed the way Sarah saw him. She became jealous, which made her more showy about being with him, which was counterintuitive to her intentions. She posted him all over her socials and hung off him at parties and around school. He pulled away from her to get away from all the attention and the gossip. It wasn't until after they broke up that he realized somewhere along the way, he'd fallen in love with the version of Sarah that existed before curious onlookers knew who they were. After they broke up, A.J. sank back into high school anonymity for nearly a year.

Jane Barrington took quiet notice of A.J. in the bleachers of a school assembly. He was handsome for a boy who sat alone. He didn't talk to anyone around him and didn't seem bothered by his lack of status. She got brave enough to approach him at a party a few weeks later.

Jane now watched eagle-eyed as Sarah rose from her seat and began walking toward the washrooms. She waited a few seconds to follow. Hovering by the entryway tile, she observed Sarah slipping into a stall before she went all the way into the hollow fluorescent space. Jane fetched lip gloss out of her bag and stared at her reflection in the mirrored wall.

Sarah emerged from the stall moments later, meeting eyes with Jane in the mirror.

"That's a really nice dress," Jane said.

"Thanks," Sarah quietly replied. "Yours is nice too."

Sarah washed her hands quickly, hoping the sound of the splashing water would dissuade Jane from any further attempt to chat.

When the tap went off, Jane continued. "Are you and Alex having a good time?"

"We don't need to do this," Sarah said, turning slightly toward her.

"Do what?" Jane asked, continuing to look at Sarah through the mirror.

"We don't need to make small talk here in the bathroom, Jane. Have a nice night."

"I didn't do anything wrong, you know," Jane said, calling out to her. "He was single, I was single. You can't be mad at me for falling for him. You obviously can relate."

"Yeah, maybe," Sarah conceded. "But, I'd never paint someone's street."

"I thought he needed something big. Something that would prove to him and to the rest of the school that I was serious about him."

"If you knew A.J. at all, you would know that the last thing he would ever want is to be included in anything so…public."

"It doesn't matter now," Jane said. "It only paved the way for Owen and me." She smoothed the side of her hair and found Sarah's eyes in the mirror again. "You and Owen know each other, don't you?"

"Everyone knows Owen," she answered. "He's gotten a lot of attention for getting drafted to the Mooseheads."

"Right," Jane said quickly, "but you know that's not what I mean."

"What are you getting at?"

"Does Alex know that you fucked Owen before the two of you broke up?"

Sarah's face went pale. She stood straighter. "What are you talking about?"

"Don't bother denying it," Jane told her. "I heard it ages ago and Owen confirmed it to me himself. And, if you remember, he's not the best at keeping his phone screen locked, so I got a chance to see the two of you in action."

"You're lying," Sarah said, her shaky jaw betraying her.

"I had a feeling there would be some video evidence after he asked to record me one night," Jane went on. "I said no immediately. But the two of you were quite impressive. Although I would've chosen a better angle to film at. That's just me."

Sarah's eyes remained fixed on Jane.

"You'll be happy to know that Alex and I never filmed ourselves. Or maybe you'd be into that, I don't know. Either way, I'm not that stupid. I'd never want to risk something like that getting into the wrong hands." Jane put a palm over her own cell phone that was resting face down on the counter.

"You're disturbed," Sarah whispered.

"Maybe," Jane casually agreed.

"A.J. doesn't want you," Sarah declared. "Owen probably doesn't either. Is this something you're going to make a habit of now? Sleeping with everyone I sleep with?" She walked a pace closer, leaning in. "Maybe you're into that, I don't know."

"Just the ones who haunt you," Jane said, shifting her weight and holding onto the counter with one hand. "I could get any guy in this school."

"A.J. knows about Owen," Sarah blurted. "Whatever you think you're doing isn't going to work."

"You think you know him so well," Jane stated.

"I know him better than you ever will. I was his first. He was mine too. There's a history between us that you could never touch."

"Alex and I have our own history," Jane said weakly. "He doesn't even know."

"Whatever happened between you two is none of my business."

Jane lifted her chin, a spark igniting in her eyes as she drew breath to speak. "It would've been everyone's business by fall if I didn't have a miscarriage."

"What?" Sarah whispered.

Jane paused, as if the weight of what she'd said surprised even herself. "I'm serious."

Something in Jane's dark, sorrowful eyes made Sarah believe her. Guilt, shame, and a long-held burden finally slipping free, even if in the most unconventional way.

"Why are you telling me?" Sarah asked. "What do you want me to do with this information?"

"I never got a chance to tell him because I wasn't sure until after I lost it."

"This isn't my secret to tell," Sarah told her, relaxing her guard.

"He doesn't want to talk to me. You don't have to tell him. Do what you want. But I do know him. And he knows me."

"I'm going back out," Sarah said. She was still shaking her head as she walked around Jane, praying she could rid the shock from her face before she returned to the table.

A.J. looked up as Sarah approached and knew before she even reached him that something had changed.

PART 4: RISING ACTION

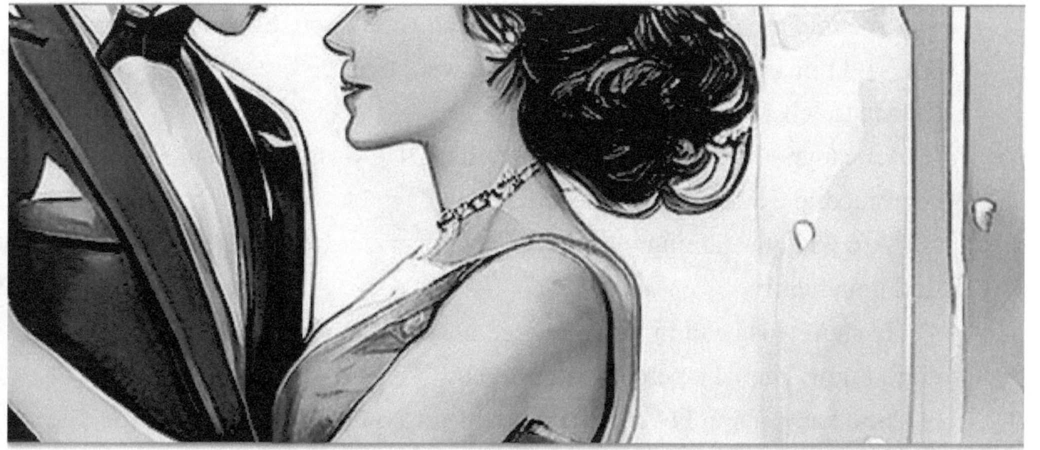

Chapter 31: A LAST DANCE

June 20th, 2025

Sarah took her seat at the table and faced him, smiling to hide the fact that she'd gone as white as the linen at their lap.

A.J. asked, "Do you want to dance?"

"Sure," she answered.

They proceeded light-footed and unsure toward the dance floor where other couples had sparsely returned. The disco ball spun slowly, dangling from the gymnasium rafters and throwing small orbs of light against the walls around them. A haunting male falsetto emerged on top of a slow languid melody as A.J. held Sarah's hips while the couple began to sway.

AKA Lisa hadn't yet reached the chorus of *Cope* when Sarah blurted out, "I saw Jane Barrington in the bathroom."

A.J. raised his eyebrows, his face silently asking whether he should be concerned.

"She told me that she had been pregnant… By you. She miscarried. She said things between the two of you were over before she got the chance to tell you."

A.J. stopped dancing, stopped breathing. He wasn't even sure if he continued to exist. "What?" he exhaled.

"Are you questioning what I told you, or what she told me?" Sarah said impatiently.

He shook his head in tiny motions, uncontrollably it seemed. "I don't know," he whispered. "I don't know."

"She knew about Owen. She thought she could blackmail me with it or something."

His eyes went dark and wild with rage. Sarah had only told A.J. about Owen a week ago. He didn't want to be reminded of it now, and he most definitely didn't want Jane throwing a spotlight on it.

"Isn't she dating him?" A.J. managed to get out.

Sarah answered, "Yes, it makes sense now why."

"This is so messed up," Alex said. He began to picture babies. A baby that looked a bit like him, a bit like Jane. Visions of suburban domesticity flooded his consciousness as if his brain was flipping through the carousel of an almost life.

Sarah reached for his arms, placing them back at her waist. She started to move again, encouraging him to join her. They danced even slower than before, barely keeping time with the music. "I can't do this," Sarah told him. "I think I should go after this dance."

"You can't leave," he protested. "This is your prom."

"I can't stay. Not with this thing hanging over us."

"We don't even know if it's true."

"It's almost worse if it isn't. It means she's willing to go to extreme lengths to get your attention."

"What do you want me to do?" Alex asked. "Should I confront her?"

"You can do whatever you think is the best thing for you. For me, I think the best thing would be if I went home."

"I don't think that's the best thing. I'll have to talk to Jane about this at some point, but Sarah, we can get through the night. We can figure this out."

"We were crazy to think that we could just pick up where we left off because half the school thought we should."

"We're not together because of them."

"I got caught up in Jane's hard launch failure too, A.J. I was brought into the whole thing for reasons I still don't completely understand."

"Do you want to go outside for a minute and talk? We could leave together. I'll get us a room for the night or something."

"No," she answered quickly. "I don't think there's much else to talk about. We've outgrown each other. That's all this is."

"I haven't outgrown you," he said. "Sarah, I love you," he said, quieter, closer to her face, reaching his hand up from her hip to grasp onto her shoulder.

She smiled. "I think you love the idea of us. Or the memories of us. That summer. The night you kissed me. The year we spent afterwards, trembling when we touched each other until we were finally tired of waiting for the perfect time."

"You want to throw all that away?"

"Of course not. I'll remember that year for the rest of my life. I'll remember *you* for the rest of my life, A.J. But we can't go off to university trying to chase a high that peaked two years ago. It'll never work. We won't even be at the same school."

"We'll both still be in the city. MSVU isn't that far from Dal."

"They might as well be a world apart. That's how it will feel."

"You don't know that."A.J. wanted to prove that he was willing to show up for her in ways he wasn't able to back then, but he felt the fight in him dying. He sensed his willingness to prove her wrong waning as the validity of her argument strengthened.

"We both know that," Sarah claimed. "I'm glad you honoured your promise to take me to prom. I wasn't planning on holding you to it."

"The night before we started high school, you made me swear we'd finish it together…at prom."

"Don't make this harder than it is," she whispered, her eyes glossing from nostalgia. "Can you walk me out?"

He nodded before he took her hand, following her off the dance floor and then outside while they waited in near silence for separate Ubers to arrive.

Chapter 32: A TRAGIC THING

June 20th, 2025

A.J. stared at the line on his screen mapping the route the driver would take to the school. He kept his free hand in his pocket and thought about drafting a message to Sarah while he waited the nine minutes that remained. Something to perhaps make her feel better as she rode home on her prom night alone. It had been at her own insistence, but A.J. still felt he was owed the blame.

He wasn't expecting to break up with Sarah before the evening ended; he wasn't even entirely sure that they were together enough to consider this a breakup.

It still hurt.

Knowing he couldn't kiss her, touch her, sleep with her tonight. Knowing he couldn't text her in the morning, or any morning. Would they still be friends the way they came to be after their first breakup?

A.J. doubted that their friendship would have respawned the way it had this time if he'd have known about Owen Shaw back then.

He heard the school doors swoosh open and a clacking pattern of footsteps quickly approaching from behind. A.J. wasn't ready to look up and confirm what he already knew in his mind.

She waited slightly behind him, dragging out the suspense. He didn't turn back, and she didn't make a move to advance ahead and be seen. He wondered how long he could stay like this. Would she be so stubborn as to continue standing there silently until his car arrived? Would he walk to the curb without looking back and get in without speaking to her? Could he be that stubborn too?

"Where's Sarah?" she finally asked in a quiet, cautious tone.

"That's none of your business," Alex replied, still staring at his phone.

"I didn't mean for things to get so…intense with her when we were talking. It just happened."

"I'm not sure I believe you. I saw you follow her. You wanted to confront her."

"You're right," Jane admitted sheepishly, stepping ahead to face him. "I'm sorry."

"Were you pregnant, Jane?"

"I think so," she told him. "I didn't take a test or anything. I was late last month. That night at the party, the night of Paint Jane, I knew there was something wrong. I knew I was later than I've ever been. I wanted to tell you, and for us to be able to figure it out together. I wanted to be with you, whether it was true or not."

"You should have told me."

"You were wasted that night. You were thinking about Sarah. I was hoping you were just confused. I thought that you needed me to prove how I felt. I thought that if I could find some way to prove it, you'd believe me. Then I could tell you what was going on, that I was late. Then we'd decide on what to do."

"Were you thinking about keeping it?"

"I don't know," she answered. "Maybe. Probably not."

"If you had come to me with this, I could have been there for you."

"I wanted to know that you cared about me without some tragic thing attached to it. I didn't want your pity after everything blew up."

"Jane," he breathed, stepping in closer to her with nothing prepared to say.

"A few days later, I…it happened. It was different than my normal periods and it lasted a lot longer. I did a few Google searches…It was…pretty unmistakable."

"Did you tell anyone?"

"Telling Sarah was the first time I've said it out loud. I think I just needed to say it. I didn't go into the bathroom planning to tell her. I just felt like I had to show her that you and I weren't just messing around. There was more to it. At least, there was for me, especially at the end."

"Are you… I mean, is everything…alright?" he stammered.

Jane shrugged through a slow blink, unsure of how to answer.

"You're with Owen now," Alex stated. "Are you two…happy?"

"Does it matter to you if I'm happy with another guy, Alex?"

"He's not my favourite person, but I hope you're getting what you need from the relationship."

Jane laughed before looking up to find Alex's eyes. She locked in on him and forced a memory of the two of them together to jump from her mind into his.

"Getting what I need," she repeated in a whisper. "What do you think I need?"

Headlights abruptly landed on the wall behind them as a car pulled into the lot. "You need to get back inside to your date," Alex said. "My car's here. I'm going home."

He smiled faintly before turning to go to the curb.

"Take me with you," she called out.

Alex stood at the backseat car door, one leg poised to get in. He heard her pleading request and knew he should ignore it. But the desperation in her posture was unlike anything he'd seen from her.

Her face held a begging pout she couldn't hide. She drew nervous breaths while she waited for his response.

He didn't know what made him step back from the car, but he moved to the other side of the door, opening it wider before glancing up at Jane.

"Get in."

Chapter 33: A FULL CIRCLE

June 20th, 2025

She slid in a bit closer to him in the back seat and asked, "Where are we going?"

"I told you, I'm going home," he reminded her.

"You're taking me to your house?" she mocked, as though she didn't believe him.

"My car is there. I'll drive you to your house."

"I was hoping we could hang out for a bit," she told him.

"And do what?"

She set her hand on his thigh. "I dunno. I'm sure we could figure out something."

"What about your stuff? Do you have a purse or anything?"

"I've got my phone," she said, holding it out in her palm. "I'll tell Owen to give my purse to Emily."

"Why did you want to leave with me?" Alex wondered.

"I think the question you should be asking yourself is why you let me?"

"Because I care about you."

"I think it's more than that."

"It's too complicated to be more than that."

"It's not as complicated as you think," Jane asserted.

"Did you forget about our parents?"

"Did you forget that I don't care about them? Let them sort their own shit out, Alex. If you care so much about me, why does it matter what may or may not have happened between our parents?"

He went silent for a beat. "I have this feeling," he began, "that I was the reason they never had their chance."

"It's not your fault that your mom and dad had sex, Alex."

"No, I know that, but there's always been this…tension with my parents when they speak about each other. Like they were forced into something neither one of them really wanted. That could have only been because of me."

"You don't know that," Jane told him.

"That day, the paint day, after you left, I came out of my room and they were still talking—your dad and my mom."

"What were they saying?"

"In that moment, nothing. But it felt like I'd walked in on something pretty intense. I don't know how to describe it. How could two people who aren't even speaking fill a room with that much… emotion?"

"I saw that in the store when they first noticed one another. I thought it was just because they hadn't seen each other in a while, but there was something more to it."

"I didn't think that you and I being around one another was helping things," he stated.

She said laughing, "Did you think that getting back together with Sarah would fix it?"

"Maybe," he confessed.

"What now?" Jane whispered.

"I take you home," he said, repeating his intentions, believing them a little less than he had before.

"What if I don't want to go home?" she posed, burrowing into his side.

"I never said it was what *I* wanted," Alex admitted, his words coming out coarse and uneven. "It's just the right thing to do."

"Who made you the moral authority in this circumstance?"

"No one," he answered, allowing Jane to place her hand on the back of his neck, gently coaxing his face toward hers. "This is an impossible circumstance," he said. "I don't see an easy way around it."

"Maybe…" she said breathily, "maybe it's better to just go *through* it."

Alex locked onto Jane's eyes, neither of them daring to break their determined gaze.

He thought about pulling away first, but instead, whispered, "I hope you're right," as he leaned in to kiss her.

Chapter 34: A QUIET COLLISION

June 21st, 2025

Abby woke abruptly, intensely aware of the hot spot her cheek had left on his chest. It wasn't light out yet, but hints of dawn crept along the far edges of skyline beyond the limits of the living room window. She didn't move, other than to lift her eyelids. She needed a moment to register what parts of the preceding hours were real. Josh was there, breathing in a peaceful rhythm beside her. That part was real. It was warm and wonderful.

She coursed through her memories, tossing out the complications that would normally arise alongside her desire for Josh. She had an unbearable urge to lift her free arm and run her hand along his torso. She longed to own this time with him, to own a part of him. To finally declare him as her own.

He stirred under her soft touch, not opening his eyes. The arm that had been draped around her suddenly tightened its hold. She glanced up at him and found his warm, steady brown eyes quietly assuring her it was okay to want him. Without a word, their mouths found each other in a quiet collision. An all-consuming implosion of a kiss carried on as they collapsed further into one another, feverishly gasping, hungrily absorbing a moment that had been denied for long enough.

They were each other now, each other then, and simultaneously a version of themselves that they never got the chance to be. They were all of those things while he ran his hand through her hair, while she held on to his back underneath his T-shirt. She was seventeen again as they barrelled up the stairs, passing the master bedroom and choosing instead to fall onto the guest bed in her teenage bedroom.

It was the beauty of their first time mixed with the skilled fervency of their last time together. It was her body, nearly forty, aged almost twenty years since he'd touched it last. Sun spots and faint laugh lines. Grey hairs beneath salon dye. A sensible brassiere beneath a designer blouse.

He still saw her young alabaster skin, the perfect curve of her hips. His forty-one year old body solid as it had been for decades, but the strain and the pain of his work now lingered lightly beneath his skin. Those aches were dulled now, suffocated by desire while he reacquainted his body with hers.

Josh locked eyes with her beneath him, taking her in, unsure if he was looking at her in the present or the past, unsure which version of him she could see in the shadowed light of sunrise sneaking through cracks of space between the drapes. Being with her again felt like home. Like he could breathe with the full strength of his lungs. Like his vision improved, like touch was an unexplored sensation.

Her moans grew heavy as pleasure bounded through her like lightning trapped in a sealed-up jar.

Their faces pressed together, both drawing breath as if it were their last. He stilled, holding her tight as she lifted her hips toward him, her fingers digging into his back.

She lay panting below him when it was over. She held onto him, already missing the motion of his body with hers. He kissed her gently on the mouth before he turned onto his back beside her.

He smiled at her, delirious with a joy that made the room blur.

She smiled back at him, the shock of how different he looked at this age softened by the ease of how familiar he still felt, even after so long apart.

"You know, if I was my twenty-year-old self, we'd already be going again," he laughed.

"Don't be silly," she replied, stroking his damp hair and basking in the redolence of his sweat, "we'd have fought first."

"Right," he conceded. "The only two things we're good at."

"Exactly," she said, pressing his head to her chest. "Lie down on me," she told him.

"I'll crush you," he said, peering up at her.

She pressed him to her more insistently this time. "No you won't. Hold me just like this. I don't know how long we'll get. Lie down on me."

"Okay," he said, acquiescing. "But Abby?"

"Yeah?" she whispered.

He kissed her chest and found her eyes once more. "This time it's different."

Chapter 35: A RED EYE

June 20th, 2025

Andrea slammed her bedroom door before slamming her back against the hard wooden surface and sliding down against it toward the floor. The impact took her breath away for a second. She was too fed up to cry, too angry at herself to give any more tears to Joshua Stone.

She locked the door and quickly changed into an oversized T-shirt and shorts before crawling into bed. Josh wasn't permitted to sleep anywhere near her tonight, though she had her doubts that he'd even try. It was useless to want him to come to her. Even if he did, even if he tried to convince her, or himself for that matter, that they could survive this interruption to their life together, it would only be temporary.

Him knowing *she* was there, not far away, at that house, a house he called home for a time, would never ease in his mind. He'd always want to go to her. He'd always wish he fought harder for her. He'd always love her more.

Love *her*, period.

* * *

Benjamin Hayes sat anxiously on a padded leather chair stool in a hotel bar, swigging from an expensive glass of rum and Coke. He was exhausted and should never have agreed to meet someone for a drink at this hour. The jet lag may have worn off, but that didn't make a social engagement at ten o'clock at night sit with him any easier.

It was the end of his fifth day in Toronto as an exhibitor in the National Home Show. He was staying in the city into next week to follow up on some conversations and meetings that had taken place during a successful round of networking.

A gorgeous woman had slipped him her card before lunch that morning while he was in discussions with a green building expert from a few booths over. Noted on the back, it just said, *10 pm, dbar.* Luckily for Ben, he was already staying at the Four Seasons, so the commute down to the lobby wasn't too much of an inconvenience for him. The timing on the other hand, remained bothersome. As was the fact that he had yet to determine if this was a business proposition or a date.

He'd simply taken the card from the stealth woman and smiled, realizing later when he flipped the card over that his smile likely indicated an agreement to her written demand. So, here he was, at 10:01, still suffering under the confines of the suit he'd been wearing all day, sipping on a cocktail that he could've gotten at Kelly's for a fraction of the price, scrolling through LinkedIn, wondering how the rest of his night would transpire.

The energetic sounds of Friday night footsteps thumped in scrambled patterns all around him, but a measured pace of stilettos on natural stone floors caught Ben's attention as the echoed clicks got closer.

The intimidating black-haired woman stood to Ben's side, wearing a maroon pencil skirt suit that clung impeccably to her curves. She set a hand on his back to signal she'd arrived, announcing over his shoulder, "I've been following you for a while."

Ben's eyes tracked her as she came around, taking a seat at the bar next to him. His expression must have appeared as befuddled as he felt.

"Your work," she corrected. "I should have said I've been following your work."

"Ah," Ben registered. "I got a bit excited for a second at the prospect of having a stalker."

"We're connected on LinkedIn," she informed him, glancing down at his phone.

"Oh," Ben acknowledged. "I wish I was a bit better at all this, but I have to admit, I don't really run my own social media. I've got a couple of much younger, cooler people who do that for me. I'm lucky they let me look at it."

"Well, I'm a fan of the work you do at Gateway. The homes you build are beautiful."

"Thank you…Isabel, right?"

"Yes. I suppose I ought to officially introduce myself," she said confidently, outstretching her hand to shake his. "I'm Isabel Sharma."

"Well, Isabel Sharma, would you like a drink?" Ben asked, signalling the bartender.

"Yes, please." She sighed with notable relief. "Technically, I'm the one who asked you here," she added, "but I see you've already gotten a drink."

"If I'm not early, I'm late," Ben explained. "My father was in the military. His obsession with punctuality rubbed off on me."

"I bet you often come in early on building deadlines," Isabel presumed.

"I'm never late," Ben replied.

"That's got to be good for business," she said.

"It hasn't steered me wrong," he agreed, returning her flirtatious tone.

They both paused when the bartender approached them. Isabel ordered an espresso martini, and Ben quickly signalled to put it on his tab.

"Thanks," she mouthed, acknowledging the gesture. "I guess you're probably wondering why I summoned you here on the off chance you were remaining in town."

"My curiosity is piqued," Ben told her.

"Mine too," she said. "I'm curious to know if you have any plans for expansion. It's my understanding that you haven't done projects outside of Alberta."

"That's correct. Operating outside of the province opens up a whole host of issues with permits and certifications."

"What if I told you I could help with all that. I had a hunch about your reasons for remaining fairly local. One of the things my company specializes in is permitting services. If you partner with us, you could bid on development projects all over the country. You could expand, franchise even."

"Are you pitching me right now?" Ben asked, taking a drink.

"Maybe, but that depends on whether it's working," she answered. "If it's not, I'll just claim I was shooting my shot with the handsome CEO of Gateway Homes."

"Flattery will get you everywhere," Ben joked, before he realized that getting a head start on his drink was making him sound unprofessional. He switched back to being more business-minded. "It's not something that was on my radar, if I'm being honest. I like the size of Gateway. We've grown at a manageable rate over the last couple of decades. I wouldn't want to risk our reputation with a surge of capability that we weren't ready for."

"I understand that," Isabel said. "Is it something you'd consider entertaining, like say, at an informal lunch meeting with my partners tomorrow?"

"If I say no, does that mean we get to explore your backup reason for approaching me?" So much for professionalism.

Isabel daringly reached out, placing a light touch on his hand. "Who says we can't explore both?"

He felt a vibration from inside his suit jacket pocket. "I like the way you think," Ben responded, fetching the phone to see who was contacting him at this hour. Even in Edmonton, it was past the close of business. Plus, it was Friday night, and a fair number of his employees would already be a few beers in at Kelly's.

Glancing at the caller ID, Ben's casually amorous disposition swiftly morphed into something else entirely. "Excuse me for a minute," he said to Isabel, jumping down from his stool. "I've got to get this."

He snuck around a corner to read the message from Andrea, knowing that if she was contacting him this late at night, it was because something serious had occurred. Something that had no doubt compounded since the last time they spoke.

Andrea: I'm ending things with Josh. I can't do this anymore.

Ben motioned to reply right away.

Ben: What happened? Are you alright? Is Janey okay?

Andrea: Janey and I are fine. I just know it's over. I can't stay in this any longer, Ben. I'm done.

Ben: Why don't you and Janey come out west for a while this summer? It might be good for you both to get away. You could stay with me for as long as you like.

Andrea: I can't run away. I'm sorry to bother you. I shouldn't have messaged you while I'm still trying to figure things out. I'll call you when I know more. I'm just nervous.

* * *

Andrea tossed her phone onto the nightstand. What had she been expecting? She was ten minutes past the biggest decision of her life and already reaching for Ben? Was she stumbling into old patterns, or ready to admit that it was Ben she wanted all along? She knew she didn't need to rope Ben into the death of her relationship with Josh. It would only give Josh reason to believe that his predilection for Abby was somehow justified.

She'd sleep on it. She'd let Josh sleep on it, too. In the morning, she would talk to Josh and calmly explain that he was truly free to go.

Next week, she would speak to Ben and hope to convey sincerely how much she regretted how things had turned out between them. She would admit to the abortion she had after their affair. She would explain to Ben that ending their affair didn't save her family, as he had hoped, and cutting her out of his life didn't make it easier for Josh to forgive her.

She'd discovered she was pregnant at the same time Ben decided on a trip to Central America, with limited cellular service.

He thought the trip would help him clear his head and resolve his feelings for a woman who belonged to a man he had once called a friend.

She would have to tell Ben the truth. Josh only agreed to take her back after the affair because he didn't want her to raise another baby on her own. Only, his willingness to step in once again made her so disgusted with herself that she had an abortion before her first trimester was over. Could Ben forgive her? Josh never could.

Andrea never understood how Josh could so deeply mourn the loss of another man's baby. She couldn't comprehend why he was willing to raise a child that would serve as a reminder of the wrong she had done. Perhaps he hated that she'd made the decision on her own. Maybe he hated all of it.

The only thing he didn't hate was being a dad, and perhaps he despised her for taking that opportunity away from him. Would Ben hate her if he knew the truth? It was a risk she was now willing to take. She couldn't continue living with this truth alongside Josh any longer. She couldn't keep hiding things from Ben.

She'd sleep on it and find a way to fix everything in the morning.

* * *

Ben: Nervous about what, Andrea?

Ben: Nervous about what?

"I'm so sorry, Isabel, but something's come up," Ben announced, short of breath when he returned to the bar. "I'm going to have to take a rain check on that meeting. I've got to fly out tonight."

"Oh, I'm sorry to hear that," she said. "You're flying back to Edmonton now?"

"Not exactly," he answered, too distracted to make up a lie. "I've got to catch a red-eye to Halifax."

Chapter 36: A NEW ARRANGEMENT

June 20th, 2025

The house was empty when they crept inside. Alex held Jane's hand, leading her through the darkness of the foyer, stopping by the fridge to grab a couple of bottles of water, and continuing down the hall to his bedroom.

She closed his door behind them and sat on his bed to undo the small buckle on the ankle strap of her stilettos.

"Do you want something of mine to wear?" he offered.

"You want me to wear clothes right now?" she countered slyly.

Alex gave her a quizzical look, almost scolding her. "I told you I shouldn't have kissed you, Jane. I got carried away and I'm sorry."

"You have to stop convincing yourself that it's wrong to want me," she told him.

"It's wrong for us to want each other," he corrected. "Besides," he continued, "I think you like the taboo of it all more than anything.

First, it was sneaking around so people at school wouldn't find out, now it's this new layer with Josh and my mom."

Jane laughed as she stood up from the bed, dangling her shoes from their straps before placing them neatly on the floor near his desk. "I don't get off on the idea of having some sexy step-sibling connection to you."

"That's not exactly what I meant," Alex replied. "But I do think that part of you enjoys how messy this is."

"Life is messy, Alex."

"No kidding."

"When are you going to accept that I actually caught feelings for you somewhere along the way?"

"Did you 'catch feelings' for Owen Shaw too?"

"Are you jealous?" she asked, her pitch curious.

"A little," he admitted.

"I don't like Owen like that. He was a nice distraction, and he turned out to be a valuable asset for my research, but I'm barely attracted to him. Not like I am to you."

"I'm still reeling from what you told me earlier. What you told Sarah. You shouldn't have brought her into this."

"She's not right for you. Don't you think there's a reason that you're here with me right now instead of her? I didn't want you pouring more time into a relationship that's just an illusion."

"You don't get to decide things like that about my life."

"I know, I'm sorry. Maybe it was the pregnancy hormones," she offered jokingly.

"That's not funny," Alex warned. "You should have come to me about that."

"It would have made things even harder."

"You wouldn't have had to go through it alone."

"I was afraid that telling you would only create more distance between us."

"What do you mean? You know that I would have been there for you. No matter the outcome in the end."

"I know. But I knew it would change things between us. Even now, I can see it. You're hesitant about me. About us. Maybe you're afraid it could happen again."

"That's not why I'm hesitant, Jane. If anything, this bonds us in a pretty remarkable way."

"Not remarkable enough," Jane huffed.

"How can you say that?"

"Because nothing came of it," she said coldly.

"Did you want something to come of it?"

"Did I want to give birth to your child during my senior year of high school?" she said. "No, of course not. But I don't want to end things entirely because that could have been a possibility."

"That's not why I think we shouldn't date anymore."

"We never dated, Alex. We had sex. A lot. For a few months."

"Thanks for clearing that up," he sighed, shaking his head.

Jane perched herself confidently on the edge of Alex's desk as he remained standing a few feet from her. He'd taken off his tuxedo jacket and began unbuttoning his shirt.

"Every guy has an Andrea and an Abby," Jane proffered. "The one who fills a void, and one who causes it."

"That's them, Jane. It's not us."

"History tends to repeat itself, especially when there's no resolution the first time around."

"We don't need to repeat it. We can choose to do something different."

"Like what?" she chuckled.

Alex yanked the remaining tuck of his shirt out from the waist of his pants. He stilled himself before suggesting with a sudden rush of sincerity that brought his voice to a soothing cadence, "We could try being friends."

"What does that do for either of us?" Jane asked.

"It gives you a soft place to land when things get heavy or uncertain."

"Who says I need that in my life?"

"I think you need it more than most people," he answered gingerly, stepping in closer.

"And what does this new arrangement do for you?" Jane whispered nervously, uncomfortably aware of how seen she felt by him in that moment.

"It's not an arrangement, it's a friendship. And it allows me to keep you in my life without the risk of complication, or," he paused, tilting his head to look up at her from under his brow, "heartbreak."

"As if you'd ever give me enough of your heart to break it, Alexander Bouchard."

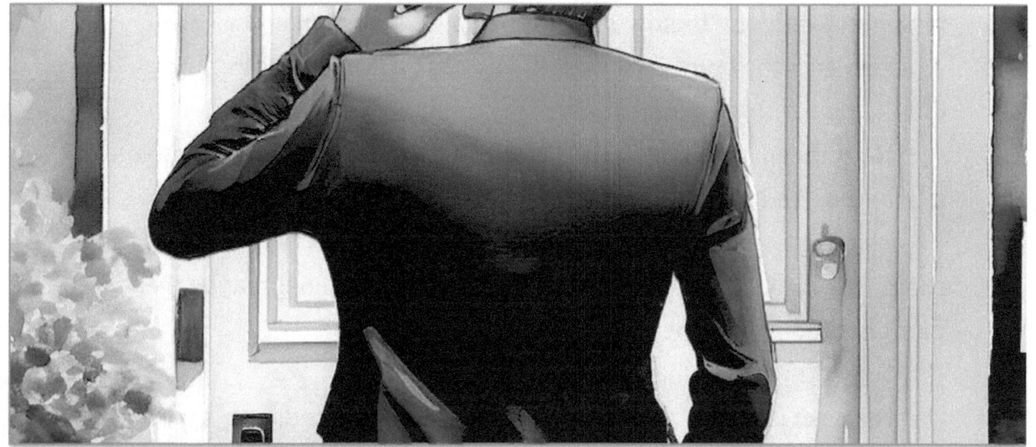

Chapter 37: AN UNEARNED HANGOVER

June 21st, 2025

She was drawn out of an incoherent dream to the sound of her cell buzzing against the nightstand. Reality set in like an unearned hangover when Andrea saw it was Benjamin Hayes on the line.

"Hello?" she whispered hoarsely.

"Are you alright?" he asked, releasing his words quickly through shallow breaths. "I was worried. Your last message was…cryptic."

"What do you mean, cryptic?" she rebuffed. "I'm sorry I pulled you into this last night, Ben. I've got to talk to Josh before I involve you any further."

"That might be difficult," Ben told her.

Andrea got out of bed and pulled her grey cotton robe from a hook on the back of her bedroom door. She slipped her arms through and tied the belt snuggly at her waist while holding the phone to her ear with her shoulder. "I know it won't be an easy conversation," she whispered as she crept into the hallway outside of her room. "We didn't leave things in a great place last night."

"No, I mean, it might be difficult for you to talk to him before you talk to me, Andy."

Andrea entered the living room only to find that it was empty. The room was cold, stale. Maybe Josh was in his workshop, maybe the guest bedroom. But she didn't think so.

"Why do you say that?" she asked weakly.

"Because I'm here. I'm at your door right now. And Josh's truck is gone."

Andrea froze in place in the living room. She tilted her head slightly to focus her gaze on the spot in the driveway visible through the oversized south-facing window. The truck wasn't where it had been parked last night when they arrived home. She raced to the entryway, still holding the phone to her ear, still hearing Ben's breathing on the end of the line. She tossed the door open to find him standing there, waiting for her, relieved to see her, then slouching with a bit of trepidation while he waited for her reaction.

"What are you doing here, Ben?" she finally let out as the arm that was holding her cell phone fell slowly to her side.

"I didn't like that message you sent me last night. I messaged a few times, tried to call. You said you were nervous, Andy. Nervous about what? About Josh?"

"I'm nervous about starting my life over. I took a sleeping pill. I fell asleep. I told you I'd call you when this blows over. I can't believe you got on a plane."

"I was in Toronto," he explained. "I had to know that you were okay."

"I'll be fine, Ben," she said unconvincingly.

"Where's Josh?"

"I don't know," she admitted. "I didn't know he wasn't home until now."

"Are you two really over?"

"Yes," she maintained. She looked past Ben at the driveway, taking in once again the absence of Josh's truck, the absence of him in the house. Letting the acceptance of knowing where he was set in.

"I've missed you, Andy," Ben revealed, sweeping over her with his eyes as if it only just occurred to him that he was seeing her in person for the first time in years.

Aware of his eyes on her, she instinctively tugged at her robe, adjusting it tighter across her torso.

"I've missed you too," she said reluctantly. She backed into the house and gestured for him to come inside.

Ben crossed the threshold and closed the door behind him. He surveyed the openness of the main floor. "Nice house," he said.

Andrea sighed, revealing, "It was mostly Josh."

"I can tell," Ben said, continuing to assess the craftsmanship skills of his former pupil.

"Do you want some coffee?" Andrea offered.

"Sure," he agreed. "Is Janey awake?"

"She's not home. She went to the senior prom last night. She stayed at a hotel with some friends."

"Does she have any idea about what's going on with Josh?"

"I don't know how much she knows."

"Does she know about us?"

"I don't think so," Andrea answered, hoping it was the truth.

Chapter 38: A BACKGROUND ACTOR

June 21st, 2025

They'd been dozing since dawn. It was now after seven. Late in the morning by Josh's standards. They quietly made love a second time, then burrowed into one another under the sheet while the wrens outside Abby's window sang in tune with the sunrise.

"How are you feeling?" he whispered into her hair.

"Happy," she breathed. A pause. "And a bit nervous."

"Nervous of what?" he asked, shifting in bed to get a better view of her.

"I think I'm just conditioned to be nervous after the fact," she explained, staring at the ceiling. "Any time we've been together, it's been at the risk of something else. Daylight makes it more real."

"We're not going to backpedal again."

“I’ve lived a lot of life without you, Josh,” Abby told him, shifting in the bed beside him. “After I left with A.J., it was like I had to prove to myself that I could survive without you. I wanted to call you every time things got difficult. When Christopher cheated again, when Grace’s cancer came back.”

“Where does that put us now?” he asked.

“I know myself better,” she told him. “I know more about the world and about being a mother. More about grief and how to cope with it.”

“I never wanted you to have to grieve alone,” he said.

“I had to,” Abby recalled. “But I wasn’t entirely alone,” she shared. “I started seeing a therapist after Grace died.”

Josh nodded, not wanting to pry, yet finding himself enduring a strange combination of jealousy and curiosity for this person who was privy to Abby’s most private thoughts.

“I didn’t tell her about you,” Abby confessed suddenly, “if that’s what you’re wondering.

Josh smirked. “You deceived a person you were paying to analyze your life? Or was I so insignificant that I didn’t make the cut?”

“I just didn’t want it to be about you when I didn’t even have the right words for who you are to me. It wasn’t going to bring back any of the people I’d lost.” She bit her lip as if she had to force herself to stop.

“It’s okay,” Josh said, holding her tighter.

“Believe it or not, it helped. The therapy. Even though I left out some details,” she said half-jokingly, “I got through it, and eventually, I grew stronger. I made peace with being the only one left in a family of four. I took some of that peace and applied it to you, to the memories of you. I never once believed I’d see you again. Certainly not like that, so casually in a store. I didn't think I'd become a background actor in a plot that had shifted its focus to our kids."

Josh kissed her head. "It is rather serendipitous, isn't it?"

"Mmm," she agreed.

"I never wanted to believe that our story was over," he confessed. "I kept hoping I'd bump into Grace just to have a reason to say your name out loud. I finally let it go. I figured her and Travis would have become world travellers anyhow."

A long silence fell between them. A cloud briefly covered the morning sun, creating an unsettling shadow on Abby's bedroom wall. She sat up, remaining in his arms, but a new tension had rolled in with the incoming shade.

Abby reached for Josh's face, kissing him long and slow. There was nothing urgent, no longing, no desperation. She smiled before pulling her face away. He couldn't see her, couldn't tell that her smile was looking more like one that was meant to ease the pain of a goodbye.

His eyes were still closed. He wasn't ready to join her in her land of doubt that he knew without a doubt had reared its resilient head once again. So he kept his eyes closed to remind himself of her willingness only hours ago to pretend, this time, that doubt wouldn't come. He wanted more time. More time in the blissful ignorance stage. It was too soon for them to enter into the incessant battle that plagued them every other time before.

"We should get up," she said. "A.J. might be home soon."

"It's only just past seven," Josh noted, "and it's the morning after his prom. I think we'll be safe for a little while yet. I'll go make us some coffee."

"Okay," she agreed.

Josh paused to observe her before getting out of bed. Last night had changed things, and neither of them knew what was going to happen next. They both had ideas about how the rest of their day would unfold.

Different ideas.

She had a habit of catastrophizing; he was an eternal optimist. Neither one of them was completely ready to set the day into motion, especially when there were no guarantees that they would end up with one another when night fell upon them once more.

He dressed quickly, haphazardly. Didn't even bother doing up his belt, the ends hanging unfastened at his waist. His t-shirt was sloppy and wrinkled from lying in a heap on the bedroom floor. He hadn't made an effort to tame his hair, only sweeping back a small section off his forehead when he bent down to give her a peck before he left the room.

"I'll be down in a minute," she called out.

"Don't worry," he turned back to say. "Take your time. I know where everything is."

Josh filled the coffee pot, instinctively knowing where the beans were kept, where the grinder was likely stashed away. He pulled the mugs from the cabinet and retrieved the cream from the fridge. He stood over the sink, gazing out at the familiar backyard, taking stock of all the memories available to him in that very setting. Some good, like the day he first saw her. Some not-so-good, like the day she married Christopher.

He was captured by a haze of half-formed recollections when quiet steps approached him from behind.

He coughed first. "What are you doing here?" A.J. finally asked.

Chapter 39: A CALM ACCEPTANCE

June 21st, 2025

Josh slowly turned to face Abby's son. Shoulders pulled back, his chest expanding with surprise, he summoned a deep breath and the patience required to deliver his response with the delicacy this moment now demanded.

"A.J." Josh said, "you're home."

"I live here," he snickered.

"I know. I just figured with prom and everything."

"You *just figured* what?"

"That you'd be out for the night," Josh answered quietly.

"That doesn't really explain why you're in my house, though, does it?"

Josh thought about what he could say that might assuage this predicament they were in. He thought of a few lies he could tell. He stared for a moment at this eighteen-year-old version of Christopher

Bouchard, who wore Abigail's eyes, and decided instead to softly surrender. "I think you probably have some idea of why I'm here."

"You're still in love with my mother," A.J. stated.

Josh tilted his head in a docile nod without committing his confession to words.

"And she's…still in love with you," he added.

"I believe so," Josh answered timidly.

"I know this goes back a while," A.J. said.

Josh's shoulders fell, relieved that A.J. was attempting to acknowledge the history of their situation. "It does," he confirmed, nodding more vehemently this time.

There was a silent pause between. They both needed a moment to digest their newfound understanding of one another.

"I'm not gonna get in the way of it," A.J. said.

"I appreciate that," Josh replied. "I'm sure your mom does too."

A.J. curled his lip in what transitioned into a cunning, closed-mouth smile. "It's a bit bigger than the three of us."

Josh's jaw tightened, reacting to A.J.'s subtle implication. He thought it rather audacious of the boy to bring Jane and Andrea into this right now. With teeth clenched, he begrudgingly acknowledged, "I know."

The distinct creak of A.J.'s bedroom door opening made both men turn their heads to face Jane, creeping toward them in the kitchen.

She stood back at first, not passing the threshold separating the hallway hardwood from the tile floor by the fridge. Quickly surveying her father's dishevelled appearance and the knowing looks that the two men before her barely had time to disguise, she simply called out to him to see if she had truly stumbled upon this awkward happenstance. "Dad?"

Josh quickly glanced at A.J. before his eyes found focus on his daughter, who wore loose-fitting clothes that were more size-appropriate for A.J. A far departure from the black gown she'd been wearing when he saw her last at the park. "Jane, what are you doing here?"

She chuckled before replying, "There's no way we're doing me first."

"Where's Owen?" Josh asked.

"Where's *mom*?" Jane demanded.

"Let's not do this right now, Janey. Go get your things, I'll take you home."

"Don't treat me like a child, Dad. I deserve some answers too."

"You're *my* child, Janey. I don't want you getting involved in grown-up problems."

"You can't shield me forever. I know why you're here, whether you want to admit it to me or not. I know that you and Mom haven't been in love for a while and that it's got something to do with Ben. I saw the way you look at Abby. I've never seen you look at Mom like that."

A light thud pulled everyone's attention toward the entryway. Several sets of eyes were now on Abby as she reached the main floor landing. She cautiously moved in the direction of the group, smiling politely at A.J. and then at Jane before saying to Josh, "I forgot to let you know that I don't take dairy creamer in my coffee anymore."

"The coffee's not quite ready yet," Josh informed her. "I got a bit side-tracked."

"I can see that," Abby noted. "Good morning…everyone."

"What's going on, Mom?" A.J. asked.

"It's complicated, bub," she told him.

A.J.'s stare darted briefly at Josh before he replied, "No shit."

"Hey!" Abby objected at her son. "It looks like *everyone's* got a bit of explaining to do. A.J., let's give Josh and Jane a few minutes. We can have our own conversation in the rec room."

A.J. glanced at Jane for approval, reluctant to leave her with Josh if it wasn't what she wanted. She nodded softly, permitting him to go.

Abby and A.J. disappeared down the hallway by the kitchen, passing his bedroom and a guest bathroom, before landing in the den.

She slid the barn door closed and said to him, "I didn't think you would be home. What happened last night? Where's Sarah?"

"I left prom early last night and came back here with Jane," A.J. explained. "It's complicated."

"No shit," Abby repeated. "You've been home all night?" she asked, bewildered.

"Yeah," he admitted. "We came back here, got changed, and went to bed."

Abby's head went down.

"You don't have to believe me, but it's the truth," he insisted. "Sarah and I broke up. I'm pretty sure Jane and her boyfriend broke up, or are breaking up. We're just going to be friends."

"I won't pry," Abby told him. "I just want to know that you're okay."

"I'm okay," he assured her. "Are *you* okay?"

Abby took a deep breath through her nose, slowly exhaling through her mouth as she searched for the courage to respond. "Yes," she replied. "Things with Josh have never been easy. We're…trying to figure it out."

"I don't hate him like Dad does," A.J. stated. "I just want you to be happy, Mom. You deserve it."

Abby made her way toward her grown son, her heart swelling with emotion at his profound display of understanding. With open arms, he pulled her into a warm embrace, and she nestled against his sturdy frame, wrapping her arms around his waist. In that silent moment, they found solace in each other, sharing unspoken words of comfort as the weight of the future momentarily evaporated around them.

In the kitchen, Jane had taken a seat on one of the island stools. Of all the conversations that Josh had been a part of around this island, he never envisioned that one of them would be between him and his teenage daughter. The well-aged surface beneath them, made of butcher block oak that he'd cut and sanded himself, unknowingly shaping a centrepiece for his future, reflected up at him as if each memory had been stashed away there in the grains.

"Are you having an affair?" Jane blurted.

"It's not that simple," Josh sighed through a reluctant exhale.

"Who says an affair is simple?" she quipped back. "Mom's affair wasn't simple, was it?"

"Janey," Josh breathed, glancing up at her from between sunken shoulders as he bent forward to talk at eye level. "There are things between your mom and me that you shouldn't concern yourself with. You were wrong before. I do love your mother."

"I didn't say you don't love her," she corrected. "I said you weren't *in love* with her. That you haven't been for a while. There's a difference."

"I know," he agreed.

"Are you going to leave her?" Jane's voice trembled, her eyes glistening as vulnerability washed over her features. "Leave me?"

"You're my daughter, Janey. That will never change," he said, emphatically grasping for her hand across the counter. "I'm afraid your mom and I aren't making each other happy anymore."

Jane pressed her lips together tightly before she motioned with an accepting nod.

"We fought last night," he confessed. "Coming here might not have been the smartest decision, but staying would've only made things worse. I don't want to fight anymore."

"So you and Abby…?" she whispered, her question trailing into a silent assumption.

"There's a history between us," he told her. "I thought I'd never see her again. I thought for sure I'd never be in this house again." He gestured to Jane and then to Alex down the hall. "Now it's my kid and her kid."

Jane was quick to offer, "Nothing happened with Alex." Then slowly corrected for accuracy, "Nothing happened last night."

Josh was skeptical but willing to accept her unprompted confession.

"I care about him. I might even love him. And I think he cares about me," she said. "But, we're better as friends."

Josh pondered his daughter's wise assessment. "How do you know that?"

"Because he doesn't look at me the way you look at Abby, Dad."

"Oh, kiddo," he said softly.

"We'll all be alright," she assured him.

"You think?" He smiled at her as he stood with a sudden boost of energy that his daughter's empathy had allowed.

The doorbell rang, surprising them both, drawing their synced gazes toward the entryway.

"I did," Jane whispered, "until a few seconds ago."

Chapter 40: A DANGEROUS DENOUEMENT

June 21st, 2025

When the knock came, Abby was closest to the front door. While following A.J. on their return to the kitchen, she changed direction to see who was calling at this hour.

"Are Josh and Janey here?" Andrea asked bluntly from the stoop before Abby had a chance to greet her. "I know Josh is," she went on, briefly darting her eyes toward his truck in the driveway. "Is Janey with him?"

"Yes," Abby admitted quietly. "They're both here." She glanced at the man positioned just behind Andrea; his nearness suggested an intimate bond between them. "Would you two…like to come in?" Abby offered, opening the door wider to admit them.

Andrea took a small step back. "This is Ben," she said.

Josh bolted up from where he'd been leaning on the island.

"Hi, Ben," Abby said, greeting the stranger with some hesitancy while she maintained a polite warmth.

Josh was beside Abby instantly, seeming to materialize out of thin air in the time it took her to blink.

Andrea watched Josh with barely concealed disdain. "I can't believe you're both here," she said.

"You're one to talk," Josh snapped. "What the hell is *he* doing here?"

"Hi Josh," Ben muttered.

Andrea straightened her shoulders. "I called him."

"Why?" Josh asked.

"Because he gives a shit about me, Josh," she said. There was a rasping coarseness rolling through her words, turning every syllable into something sharp.

Both men at the doorway surged toward Andrea. Josh first, perhaps to oppose her claim, not realizing that his hawkish response would only validate it. A protective instinct flared within Ben, driving him to move in before he could assess the danger Andrea faced.

"Guys," Abby said to A.J. and Jane, who had made their way to the entryway as well, "maybe you should give us a few minutes."

"I'm not going anywhere," A.J. announced, stepping in closer toward his mother as he watched these two men posturing in his home.

"We already understand enough about what's going on, Mrs. Bouchard," Jane said quietly.

Andrea looked at her daughter. "What did they tell you?"

Josh backed off, forcing hot air from his lungs. "Janey, let the adults deal with this," he said firmly.

Ben took half a cautious step forward. "Listen, Josh, I know I'm not the guy you want to see right now. Andrea sounded upset last night, and I thought she could use some…support."

"The same support you gave her ten years ago?" Josh bit back.

"What's going on?" A.J. whispered to Jane.

"My Mom and Ben had an affair," Jane told him, loud enough for everyone to share the truth.

"What?" Andrea cried. "Who told you that? Did Josh tell you?"

"No, Mom," Janey said. "I'm old enough to put the pieces together. Ben was around a lot, and then he wasn't. And he would still send me cards and gifts for birthdays and Christmases." She leaned forward, speaking more directly to her mother. "You would let me say hi when you talked to him on the phone as long as I didn't tell Dad." She paused, redirecting her gaze to Josh. "Men stop being friends over money or women. I didn't figure you two had a financial falling out, so it had to have been about Mom."

All the eyes in the room were locked on Jane. They struggled to believe she had been sorting these clues for so long.

"Oh, Jane," Andrea said, approaching her. "I'm sorry that you had to grow up knowing about things you shouldn't have. I should have… been more careful with you."

Abby noted the shock washing over Josh's face. His mouth fell open as the tension in his jaw relaxed. She watched him weigh everything that had been brought before them this morning.

Josh was fighting back reminders of fondness for his former mentor. Ben's familiar eyes were sturdily set upon him.

"Jesus Christ," Josh muttered. "You've been talking to him all these years. You two have kept up some sort of relationship? Does he know *everything*?"

Andrea felt an unsettling dread surge through her limbs. "He knows all of it," she said through gritted teeth. "I told him this morning."

"Told him what?" Jane interjected.

"Not here, Josh," Andrea pleaded, her eyes imploring him to spare Jane from learning the remaining bits of truth she wasn't meant to know. "But he does know *everything*."

"You don't love her, man," Ben quietly interrupted. "You wouldn't be *here* if you did."

"This is family business," Josh growled. "It doesn't concern you."

Ben paused, bowing his head as if he'd removed his shield at the height of battle. "I've always loved her. You know that."

Josh strode up to him, an air of resolution about him, as if he were prepared to accept an overdue apology.

But in a split second, without any hint of his true intentions, he unleashed a powerful punch that landed squarely on Ben's cheek.

A single heartbeat of silence shattered into a collective gasp as tension crackled through the room, holding everyone in stunned suspense.

Ben didn't move. He took the hit. The others stood rigid and unsure as they waited for Ben's reaction.

"Then why the fuck did you leave her, you coward?" Josh's words came out sharp, heavy with anger he'd carried for years.

Andrea took a step closer to Josh. "It wasn't his fault," she said gently. "The whole time during the affair, I was telling Ben that you and I were separated. That's why he was here in Halifax. I made him believe that you and I were over, and he came down under the pretence that I needed help to get on my feet without you." She glanced at Ben, her mouth turned down. "When Ben found out that I wasn't going to leave you, that I couldn't take Janey away from you, he left."

"But I saw you." He turned his head to Ben. "We fought. I confronted you."

"He covered for me," Andrea explained. "He thought sharing the blame could somehow make it easier for me to try and save my family."

"I'm sorry," Ben breathed out.

"I didn't find out that I was pregnant until after he was gone. I tried to get in touch with him first, but he didn't have his phone or his laptop for weeks. I never thought in a million years you would want me to keep it, Josh. Especially once I'd told you the baby was Ben's."

"You let me believe that he knew all along. That he left anyway. Then you did what you did without even talking to me first," Josh said, his voice unsteady as the details crashed over him.

"What did you do?" Jane asked.

Andrea turned to her daughter, her gaze filled with a clarity that defied explanation.

"Oh," Janey whispered.

"There," Andrea said, half sobbing, mocking indignation, "*everyone* knows *everything*."

Abby felt herself shrinking as her mind slipped into a darkening tunnel, away from the people in her foyer. She was a spectator now. She watched Josh in his own state of uncertainty, surrendering the fight as he reeled from the past.

"Neither of our hearts was ever really in this, Josh," Andrea said calmly. "It just took me a little bit longer than you to realize it." She met his eyes, relief softening her resolve. "I want to be with Ben, and he wants to be with me."

"Let her go, man," Ben pleaded softly.

Abby watched Josh's eyes hesitate on Andrea.

In that millisecond, while Josh's past and present were colliding, Abby affirmed her intuition. If she was meant to end up with Josh, their happy-ever-after wasn't meant to start today.

It would be too fresh. To go from one family to another. Too fresh like it was back then with Grace.

"Janey can finish her last year of high school in Edmonton," Andrea said.

"You can't just take my daughter," Josh objected.

"You've never adopted her. We're not married. You have no legal rights to Janey, Josh."

"Mom!" Jane cried. "You can't make huge decisions like this for me without telling me."

"You promised me you'd never do this," Josh reminded her, his heartbeat quickening again. "You said that not being her biological father would only ever be a technicality. I raised her, Andrea. You can't just take her."

"I'm not going anywhere, Dad, don't worry," Jane said.

"Yes, Janey," Andrea argued, with a gentle, coercive firmness. "I know you probably don't remember it much, but you'll like Edmonton. I'm sure you could use a change of scenery as much as I could." Her glance went to A.J. at the end.

"I'm not moving," Jane insisted. "I'll get emancipated. I'm staying here. I want to go to college here."

"You can come back when it's time to go to college," Andrea suggested. "But you'll finish high school in Edmonton first. You can fly back every couple of months to see Dad."

"No," Janey grumbled, tears building in her eyes. "I want to stay in Halifax."

Andrea let out a resigned sigh. “We’re not going to resolve every detail right now,” she said. “Why don’t you get your things and come home with us?”

“Who’s *us*?” Jane shot back. “You and Dad, or you and Ben?”

“Me and Ben for right now,” Andrea told her. “Your Dad and I need to talk at some point.” She glanced at Josh. “And then he and I will sit down with you and let you know what we’ve decided together.”

Jane made one last attempt in protest. “I’m not just going to go along with this madness.”

Andrea reached for Jane’s shoulder and made a soft, sweeping motion down the length of her arm.

A strange quiet fell over the room. No one argued anymore. No one reached for a different outcome.

“We should go, Janey,” Andrea said, exhaustion seeping through the cracks in her voice.

“Okay, Mom,” Jane obeyed. She inched, head down, toward Josh and hugged him before returning to her mother’s side.

Mom and daughter clung to one another before turning to head for the door. Ben looked at Josh before following the women. There was nothing to say. Josh gave a slight flick of his chin, a small gesture that told Ben the two men would part on cordial terms.

Abby, Josh, and Alex stood scattered across the entryway. They stared at the closed door as if a tornado had just torn through the house. Now, in the heavy silence, they were left to take stock of the wreckage it left behind.

PART 5: GOOD POINT

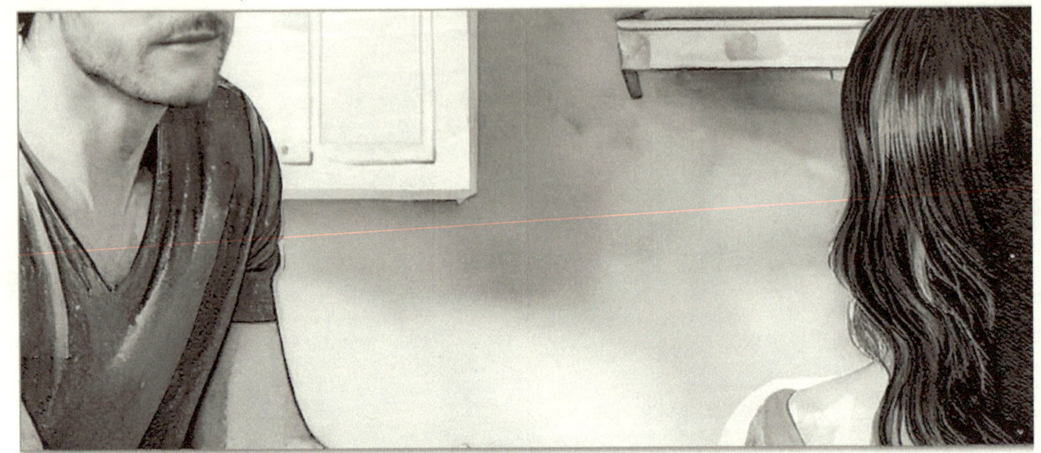

Chapter 41: A YEAR AHEAD

June 21st, 2025

A.J. broke through the quiet first. "I'll give the two of you some time," he said, walking cautiously past Josh and Abby, as if there was shattered glass on the floor.

"You don't have to leave, A.J.," Abby said. "We can talk if you want."

"It's okay, Mom, I'm good. I'll be fine," he insisted. He shot a look at Josh, but kept its meaning deliberately vague. He wasn't angry, but he wasn't offering peace either.

"Are you sure, honey?" Abby pleaded.

"Jesus, Mom. I'm sure." He put an arm around his mother, lightly squeezing her shoulders as he planted a kiss on her head. "You guys should talk."

"Don't be too long," she called out, knowing he'd be on his own clock the moment he drove away.

As the front door closed behind her son, Abby let out an enormous sigh. "I need the biggest cup of coffee," she announced, heading back toward the kitchen.

Josh followed behind her and watched intently as she picked up where he'd left off. He couldn't read Abby. She was clearly avoiding the debrief—the part where they had to dissect what had happened and what it meant for them.

"I'm sorry," Josh blurted. "I'm sorry they showed up here, and I'm sorry I lost my cool."

"It's okay," she said, her back still turned to him. "It's your family."

"You're my family too," Josh added.

"Yeah," she whispered.

"Why won't you look at me?" he asked.

She slowly turned, revealing the pale panic on her skin. The distance in her eyes. She'd already retreated. "Josh," she breathed.

Turns out it wasn't different this time.

"Don't do this," he begged, shifting his weight before his hand darted up to grab his hair. "Don't tell me you've already decided that we won't work."

"This isn't the right time for us, Josh. We both know it," she said. The grumbling sounds of brewing coffee echoed behind her, the drip steady and indifferent. The smell wafted through the steam and found her nose, reminding her that this entire exchange occurred before she'd even had any caffeine in her system.

"How can you say that?" Josh argued. "Didn't you just watch me let her go a few minutes ago? Didn't we wake up in each other's arms this morning happier than either one of us has been in years?"

"Yes," she said softly.

"So what's wrong with right now?" he said, trying to reason with her. "What else can I do to prove to you that now is as good a time as any? Maybe there will never be a *perfect* time for us, Abby. I can admit that there was some truth to the impossibility of our timing back then. We were young. I was stupid, and I wasn't making your life any easier. But we're beyond all that, aren't we? I can take care of you properly now."

"I don't need anyone to take care of me, Josh," she said. "We have to let some wounds heal before we jump back into battle."

"Battle? Abby, the battle's been won. It was hard fought by everyone, but we did it. We're here, we're still standing. There's nothing else. *No one* else keeping us apart."

"It doesn't feel like the right time to start something so…"

"So what, Abby?"

Her shoulders fell. "So…serious."

"You want to have a fling?" he asked, recoiling. "You want to be friends with benefits? You want to Netflix and chill? I can do that. I can be…" he stopped to swallow, "casual."

"No, you can't," she said. "And neither can I. I have no interest in casually dating you, Josh."

"I thought you *wanted* me," he reminded her, drawing out his words.

"I do. That hasn't changed."

"Sounds like it has," he said, tense and unrelenting. "Explain it to me, Abby. Are we just playing out our pattern? We had five minutes together where we fantasized about forever, and now that you've got the want out of your system, you're ready to toss me aside. It feels eerily familiar."

"Don't tell me how I feel, Josh. Don't get angry with me because it's easier for you to be mad when things aren't going the way you think they should."

"Jesus Christ, I'm so tired of doing this? It's exactly the same as it was seventeen years ago. And three years before that. And in a million tiny ways in the years before that."

"You brought me into this before I ever knew what these kinds of feelings were," Abby said.

"I had never been in love before I met you, Abigail." He stopped to let the weight of her full name linger on his lips. "I was just as new to it as you were."

As much as she wanted it to work, as much as her heart hammered in her chest when he said her name like that, she still resisted. "You had been with other girls before that summer, Josh. Then, after kissing me, you spent the next two years sleeping with my sister."

"Is that what we've come back to now, huh? It's not enough for you to watch my family walk away from me; you wanna bring Grace into this? If you haven't forgiven me for Grace, I don't know where to go from here."

Abby's expression softened. "I've made my peace with everything that happened with Grace."

Josh had already worked himself back up. "It doesn't fucking sound like it," he mumbled. "Do you even realize what it did to *me* when you moved away? One minute you were with me, and then you were gone. You broke my fucking heart."

"Josh," she sighed, voice low and unflinching, "you broke mine first."

"I'm here bleeding words, and promises, and devotion—everything I possibly can—to convince you to be with me." He slouched lower, growing quieter as if the fight were draining from him. "And you're looking for reasons to run."

"I didn't say never," she said. "I think I'm saying not right now."

"That's a cop out," he muttered. "Just like that letter."

"What letter? The one that Grace wrote? I didn't mean for that to happen. I didn't know she was going to do that."

"No. Not the one that Grace wrote. The one that *you* wrote. When Arthur died. The last words I ever got from you until I turned a corner in a wholesale store two months ago and saw you."

Abby took a small step back, placing herself further away from him. "You think that what I wrote to you then was a cop out?"

"You don't?"

"What else could I have said? We were over. I didn't want to be cruel and ignore the fact that you lost someone you were close to."

"I didn't want us to be over."

"I didn't either, Josh. The decision I made was about A.J. It wasn't about you or me."

"Who is it about now? Grace is gone, A.J. is grown. Christopher is out of the picture. Andrea left here with Ben." Josh crossed his arms from where he stood. "What's making you turn your back on us this time?"

"Andrea left here with Ben twenty minutes ago, Josh. She also left here with Jane," Abby said. "Jane, who spent the night with A.J." She crossed her arms, mirroring him. "You're omitting some important details."

"Those details don't change anything."

"How do you know?" she asked. "I don't know what's going on between the two of them, but I don't want to get in the way of it." Abby went closer to the island, setting her palms on the counter. "I know what it's like to be a casualty of circumstance," she said. "I don't want to be the circumstance that gets in their way."

"They're kids, Abby," he said. "They don't know what they want. I've wanted you for more than half my life. Doesn't that count for something?"

"You would sacrifice her happiness for yours? For ours?"

"No, that's not what I'm saying. If Jane and A.J. want to be together, I'm not going to stop them. I just don't think that it has any bearing on you and me."

"It would be weird for them, don't you think?"

"I don't give a shit if it's weird for them, Abby. I love you."

"I love you, too. I do. But this thing between us, it's got… attachments to too many other things in our lives. And it puts those other things at risk. We've been selfish before, and it never ends well."

"I wouldn't describe our history like that," he sulked.

"Most of the people I've loved are gone, Josh," she said, sorrow echoing through her. "It's been A.J. and me for a long time. I can't do anything that would risk pushing him away. It would kill me to not be as close to him as I am now.

"What happened last night was wonderful, but it was careless. I have this habit of being careless when I'm around you. I need to be with you in a way that's not careless. I need to be with you in a way that's *careful*. I can't do it if it puts my relationship with my son at risk, and I can't do it if it's not permanent. I can't lose you again to my own carelessness."

She paused, drawing in a rescuing breath.

"I love you," Abby said, "and I want you." She paused, then finished softly, "just not like this."

"What are you saying?" he asked, afraid her next words would cut deeper than the silence stretching between them.

She stared past him, out the kitchen window over his shoulder, into the yard. Past the patio, across the pool. She concentrated on the lounge chair, still shaded by the house at this hour of the morning, aimed away from the backyard entrance as it always had been. It was a different chair now, the one from her adolescence had rusted and been replaced a few times since the day she was recalling so vividly.

The day her life changed course.

The day Josh Stone approached her, neither of them knowing their fates would be sealed the instant their eyes met. He had no idea that he'd never again know a day when he didn't want her in some capacity. She had yet to understand that she would never experience life in the presence of another person the way she experienced it with him.

She was ready to end it. To let him walk out the door and close this chapter the way she had before.

But something shifted when she thought of the girl she had been the day he first walked into her backyard. Before funerals, before hospitals, before she understood how quickly everything could be taken.

That girl who spent a whole day in this kitchen with him back then didn't know she'd grow up measuring love by its potential cost.

Abby let herself wonder what it might mean to choose as if she were still that girl in the kitchen. Only this time, she'd choose with the wisdom of everything she'd survived.

"Let's give it a year," she finally said.

Desperation stretched across his features; his eyes narrowed, and his mouth tightened like a knot being enforced. "A year? We've tried that before, Abby."

A half-hearted laugh escaped. “Grace isn’t here to interfere this time.”

His lips pressed together in scorn. “That’s not funny.”

“It’s a little funny,” Abby said. “She would’ve found it ironic.”

“What do you think is gonna happen in a year?” Josh asked. “Are you hoping I’ll lose interest? That you will? Or that I’ll give up on us?”

“No,” she answered firmly. “A year gives the dust time to settle. I know my feelings for you won’t change, Josh. But we need some closure in our separate lives before we attempt a life together.”

“I got all the closure I needed when Andrea walked out the door with Ben,” he said.

“I doubt that.” Abby shook her head. “And it’s not just closure from her… You need closure from this version of us. I need that too. As much as I want us to be together, I want a fresh start. I want us to begin the rest of our lives… without causing a massive disruption to everyone and everything around us.”

“So, how does this work?” he asked, sounding as though he might actually consider taking part in her experiment.

“I don’t know,” she said. “Maybe we need to agree to no contact. We’ll walk away from one another now, not in anger, not in fear, or resentment, knowing that we’ll find each other when the time is right.”

His features still reflected skepticism. “And a year from now is when you see the time being right for us?”

“Maybe,” she said. “At least a year. There are some things I need to take care of. I’m sure you need to take care of some things, too.”

“And there’s no way that we can do those things together?” he tried.

“No,” she said gently.

"How do I know that you'll be there on the other end of this?"

"You don't," she answered. "That's the whole point. We're not good for each other like this, Josh. Everything is too raw. We'd end up reliving every bad decision we've ever made."

She got close enough to touch him, but kept both arms at her sides. "Take a year to focus on you. On your work, on yourself, on whatever you need to do to forgive everyone who's let you down." She paused, finally reaching out and setting her hand on his chest. "Including me."

"You've made this decision for us already, just now, haven't you?" he asked, staring down into her eyes. "Fate brought us back together. How can you argue with fate?"

"Fate comes into play after we've done the work, Josh. That's what needs to make this time different. We're older now. Wiser than before, I hope. I have to do this, and I think you'll want it too."

"What I want, Abigail, is you," he said, his voice measured, lips barely parted.

"We need to get it right this time," she said. "I need some time. I need to have a plan that isn't about running away or being afraid, or an ultimatum that someone has put on me."

"It sounds like you're running away," he said stubbornly.

"I think we'd be running away from everything that has been going on in our lives for the past couple of months if we ran toward each other right now. The same way I went to you when I didn't want to accept the truth about Christopher."

"Hmph," he puffed.

Another long, voiceless moment fell over them. He moved around the island, stretching his torso like a statue that had come to life. He began to mindlessly tidy the kitchen, putting their empty mugs in the sink, rinsing the empty coffee pot out for tomorrow. A tomorrow he wouldn't experience with Abby.

He'd been waiting over half his life for her. What was one more year?

He moved around her and then past her. To the living room where he'd kicked off his shoes by the sofa last night.

She began to wonder if he would leave her like this. No goodbye, no looking back. Maybe that was what she deserved. She'd spent most of the morning sure of her convictions, proud even of the strength she found to choose herself now if it meant that she'd finally allow herself to choose him a year from now.

But his quiet acceptance made her second-guess her resolve.

She propped herself up on the island and watched him gather his things from the side table. He put his phone in his front pocket, his wallet in the back.

He caught her movement and took strides in her direction. His mouth curled up as he remembered her just as she was now, sitting small and nervous on the counter the night of her seventeenth birthday.

She parted her knees just enough for him to step between them. Josh gripped the butcher block on either side of her, bringing his face in close.

"You shouldn't tease me before you send me away," he murmured low and slow, his breathing falling into rhythm with hers.

Her eyes found his after an indiscreet glance at his lips. "I didn't mean to."

"Yes, you did," he said.

"Meet me," she whispered, grabbing hold of his arms. "You know where. You know what time. A year from today."

He nodded, then buried his face in her neck, his lips grazing the skin hidden beneath her hair.

His thoughts tumbled over a thousand things he could say. A million ways he could beg her to change her mind. He considered a few dozen ways he could try to make her laugh once more.

Ultimately, he chose to say nothing.

He lifted his head until his eyes met hers. They stayed locked on one another, unmoving.

He blinked, disconnecting from her. Putting purpose in step, Josh walked to the front door, then lingered, glancing over his shoulder before disappearing into the mid-morning sun.

Abby gasped for air when the door clicked shut behind him. She sank down off the island and fell onto the couch when she heard his truck driving away from the house. She gripped the blanket, bringing it to her nose, praying to find remnants of his scent. She brushed the textured linen of the sofa, touching a spot his body had touched.

Lying her head on the pillow, Abby closed her eyes and bit down gently on her bottom lip, reinforcing the loss—the sharp pain of resisting one last kiss from Joshua Stone before he left.

She felt the ache of it.

The cost of choosing carefully.

Chapter 42: A LIFE'S WORTH

July 11th, 2025

She lingered in the truck a few seconds before reaching for the handle.

"You should come in," Jane said.

Josh's eyes went to Andrea's car parked in front of him. "I'm the last person your mother wants to see."

"Are you two really going to pack up the house separately and then just go your separate ways?" she asked as if it were a dare.

"It's what we agreed to, kiddo. I'll be by on Monday to get a few things out of here." He chuckled when he added, "If your mom hasn't already taken everything I own to the dump."

"She hasn't," Jane told him. She looked down at her hands. "You know…I've been thinking about what Mom said. About moving to Edmonton."

Josh turned his head to face Jane.

"At first, I thought leaving would feel like losing." She gave a small, indifferent shrug. "But maybe it's not. Maybe it's just time for something different."

It was the first time she'd spoken to him about the move without resistance. Josh clocked the shift, but didn't push for more.

"Your mom's not always wrong," he said, a soft smirk breaking through.

Jane offered him a small, acknowledging nod before turning to get out of the truck.

They saw the front door swing open and turned their heads in unison. Andrea stepped out, one hand on the door, the other on the frame. She tilted her head, one corner of her mouth lifting in a peaceful gesture. Her radiant skin, tousled updo, and loose sweats gave her an easy, approachable air.

In that moment, he realized he would miss this version of her: soft, unguarded, no longer grasping for something he couldn't give. He'd spent years chasing this version of her—the one in the doorway of their home—like a high he could never reach. In the end, not wanting him looked better on her than anything else.

"Maybe I'll come in for a second," Josh announced. "We are adults after all." He followed humbly behind Jane.

Andrea widened the doorway to let her daughter in, and Janey ducked past her with a light smile. As Josh drew nearer, Andrea pulled the door closer to her, narrowing the opening into the house.

"I thought we agreed that Monday would be your day," she said firmly, though her welcoming eyes betrayed her.

Josh cleared his throat before he said, "Janey…um, suggested I should…come in."

Andrea gave the door a light push and stepped to the side of the threshold, making room for him to enter. "I'm not going to stop you from coming into your house," she said.

"*Our* house," he quickly corrected.

"You built it," she quipped.

"For *us*, Andrea."

"And look at us now," she said under her breath.

"Do you want me to go? I'll stick to the plan," he offered. "I'll come back on Monday while you're at work."

"No," she sighed. "It's fine." She stopped in the living room in front of a pile of boxes that came up to her waist. She yanked the end of a roll of packing tape, sending a scratchy echo through the room, then patted the sticky surface on the seam of the box to seal it. "Is there something in particular that you're looking for? Everything's sort of scattered at the moment."

"No, not really," he said. "I saw you at the door, and I just didn't want to drive away yet."

She took a second to soak in his answer. "That might be one of the most honest things you've ever said to me."

"Are you happier now?" Josh asked her. "Are you relieved?"

Andrea shook her head as she was about to speak, as if part of the conversation was already well underway in her mind. "Am I happier after spending twenty years with a man who never loved me? Hmm. Am I relieved? Relieved about what, Josh? That I can finally stop begging you to love me?"

"I'm sorry," he said sheepishly. "That was stupid."

"The stupid thing is that you're right. I am relieved. It took all of this for me to realize that I needed to be let go by you to put my own life into perspective."

"What we had," Josh began, glancing at the box before his eyes went to her, "it wasn't nothing."

"I know that. You've raised Janey, and you'll always be her Dad, and I'll always be eternally grateful that you were ready and willing to do that despite everything, Josh. I may never fully understand how your heart works, but I know how big it is. You took care of us when you didn't have to, and we made a life's worth of memories together."

"Surely you know that it was more than that. I wanted this life with you. The one we built together. I wanted it more than anything."

"*Almost* anything," she corrected.

Josh sighed, guilt rushing out of him like a racing hound.

"I was just as stubborn as you were for most of it," Andrea confessed. "I punished you. I dared you to leave in a dozen different ways, and you never did. And as much as I hated myself for what I did, and the lies I felt like I had to tell to get us through it, I resented you for never leaving. What sane person would keep coming back the way you did? It wasn't until I saw you with her, and the effect she had on you, that I finally realized the only way you'd ever leave would be for her. I was your punishment. I'm the punishment you put on yourself for losing her in the first place."

"Andrea," Josh breathed, "I…"

"Don't, Josh. I'm okay. You'll be okay. Whatever's going on with you and Abby will work itself out."

"I don't know. I don't deserve either of you, and it looks like the universe is catching up to that notion."

"You two will figure it out," she said casually, so optimistic and unfeeling.

She didn't owe him any sincerity, Josh knew that. But it still surprised him that Andrea could appear so unburdened by the demise of their relationship, inevitable as it was.

"When do you fly out?" Josh asked, stepping away from the pieces of their life together, now packed in cardboard.

"Ben went back on Monday for work. Janey and I are going next Friday."

"She seems to have come around on finishing high school in Edmonton."

"I think so," Andrea agreed. "We talked a lot about it, and I think she's pleased with the thought of being in a place where she's not quite as known."

"A bit of anonymity couldn't hurt at this point," Josh said, his voice low to avoid being overheard. "I still can't imagine not seeing her every day."

"Whether it happened now, or next year when she went to college, she was always going to leave the nest, Josh. You just have to get used to it a year earlier."

"Maybe you're right. I just..." he said, trailing off and then stopping altogether. He braced himself against a dining room chair behind him, calculating the new distance between them. "I want you both to be happy is all."

She studied his face, eyes narrowing just a fraction as a faintly devious smile tugged at her lips. "Believe it or not, I want the same for you."

Chapter 43: AN ADVENTUROUS APPETITE

April 12th, 2026

The staging was flawless. Warm tones and inviting textures accented by strategic pops of colour. Everything she needed had come from the warehouse; most of her belongings were packed in storage. She kept a few family photos on the wall near the stairs.

She had booked a room at Muir, with its breathtaking view of the Halifax Harbour. The thought of watching the pink sky fade into night as ships sailed slowly past the George's Island lighthouse helped soothe her nervous stomach.

The suitcase in her car was packed with essentials for the next three weeks, and her flight was scheduled to depart before noon tomorrow. She quickly texted Morgan to confirm he'd arranged a car service to drive her to the airport. He promised to pick up her car from the hotel in the morning and take good care of it while she was away.

There was still an hour until the open house was scheduled to start, so it surprised her when the doorbell rang while she was scrolling through e-mails on her phone.

She got up to answer the door and saw him through the window on the other side. She was struck at once with joy and with sadness because seeing him brought it all back.

But she had called him.

She gave him the option to come see the house one last time, knowing it would be difficult for him, but not wanting to rob him of the opportunity to say goodbye to the place where he made memories too. Good and bad.

"It's so good to see you," she breathed out, eagerly making room for him to join her inside. "You look great! Come in, Come in. You didn't have to ring the bell. You used to live here."

"Hey, you," he said a bit shyly. He extended his arm to embrace her. Looking behind her as they let go of one another, he said, "That feels like another lifetime ago." He paused briefly. "I suppose it was."

They froze there in the entryway, both remembering.

"You seem like you're doing well," he said, smiling warmly at her. "How are you holding up with all of this? It must be hard to let this place go."

"I've spent the last little while letting a lot of things go," she told him. "This place was last on the list. It's not easy. But it's time. Alex lives downtown close to the university, and it didn't make sense for me to hold onto it any longer."

"He texts me every once in a while," he revealed. "I'm really glad he's stayed in touch. He's a smart kid. Sounds like he's enjoying school."

"Yeah, I think so. He's managed to fit a few creative writing classes into his engineering course load. I think he may be discovering that he's got more right-brain aspirations than he thought." She lightly nudged him before saying, "Maybe you had something to do with that."

"Creativity is obviously in his genes," he replied, peering all along the main level, resting his eyes for a second on a black and white photograph near the base of the stairwell.

It was a photo that Debra Conrad had taken of Grace and Abby walking hand in hand. The girls' faces weren't visible because the picture was taken from behind, but Grace's stringy blonde hair and Abby's wild toddler curls would give it away to anyone who knew the family and their history.

Abby smiled. "I'm really happy you came by," she said.

"Me too, Abs. I went back and forth. I wasn't sure if I should. I didn't know if I could even bear to bring up those memories. But I realized that most of them were good. And now that I'm a bit further removed from the bad ones, it's not so hard standing in this house again."

"I should have reached out sooner," she confessed.

"It's okay. We agreed," he said. "You knew how hard it was for me to be reminded."

She nodded, relieved that he was so quick to forgive her neglect.

"What's next for you? Do you still have your design business?"

"Yeah, I do. Well, technically, I do. I sold part of it to a managing owner. I've still got control of the majority, but he's going to run things while I'm away for a little while. I haven't even found a new place yet."

"You must be channelling your sister's appetite for adventure," he remarked.

"Maybe," Abby said. "I need to get away."

"Where are you off to?"

“Funny you should ask,” Abby said teasingly. “I was inspired by a Nat Geo article I read recently about Costa Rica.”

“Get out!” he said, arching back. “Are you serious?”

“I’ve booked the Canopy Villa at Pacuare Lodge for the rest of the month,” she said, hoping it would please him.

He chuckled and said, “Gosh, you should have told me. That’s where I stayed when I was working down there for the shoot. The owner bought some of the photos. I could have called in a favour. At least let me reach out to him and let them know you’re coming so that you get the full VIP treatment.”

“Okay,” she agreed, laughing.

“Promise me you’ll call me while you’re there if you need anything. I’ve been to Costa Rica a bunch of times. Every time I’m there, I think about how much Grace would have loved it if we had the chance to go together.”

“I promise I will. I know I’ll be thinking of her while I’m there. Of both of you. I miss her so much. I can’t believe it’s been ten years.”

“I know,” Travis agreed. “It’s still so raw somctimes.”

She wanted to cry. Abby wanted to reach out and console him because she thought he might be on the verge of tears as well. She swallowed the surge of emotion in her chest and asked, “How is Stella? And Eddy must be, what, twelve? Thirteen?”

“He’ll be thirteen next month,” Travis answered proudly, as if he were the boy’s father.

Travis had gotten remarried seven years ago to Stella Fairbanks.

“Well, you be sure to call me if you ever need any tips for parenting a teenage boy.”

“Ha, I will. You’ve done a pretty remarkable job.”

“Why, thank you,” she said, lightly blushing.

"I got lucky with Stella and Eddy. And Eddy's father is a decent guy. We get along well. Stella has a pretty amicable relationship with her ex."

"Geez, what's that like?" Abby joked.

"How is Christopher?"

"He's Christopher. He seems happy with his new wife, and he's good to A.J. That's all I can ask for at this point. It's so great that you found someone."

"Look at us," he said, gesturing at her shoulder, "all grown up."

"Yeah," she sighed.

"You know, Stella and I were at a dinner party with some friends a few months ago, and there was this beautiful live-edge dining table. She asked who made it, and the owner of the house said that it was a custom piece by Markham Stone. I Googled the business, and it turned out to be an architectural firm that designs homes and custom furniture. Part owner and Lead Carpenter listed as none other than Joshua Stone."

"Was this Ethan Charles' home?" Abby asked.

"Yeah, do you know him?"

"Yes," she admitted. "I did the interior design of his home."

"No way! I should have known. It felt a bit like you in there."

She managed a shy smile. "I was seeing Ethan for a while."

"What a small world," Travis said, a bit bemused by the connection. "So you and Josh… are in touch? You worked on the home together?"

"Oh gosh. It's a long story. It is indeed a very small world, though. I asked his mother to essentially come out of retirement to sell this house. I just saw her pull in."

Travis chuckled. "We really do need to catch up more often."

"I would love that, Trav."

"Me too. Why don't you and Alex come for dinner at the house with Stel and me? And Eddy. I wanna hear all about Costa Rica when you get back, and about Alex's first year of University. I'm not saying this in a polite, never follow through, kind of way either. I want to see you guys more often."

"Of course. I'll call you when I get back. If not sooner, from the jungles of Central America."

"I'll hold you to it."

"I hope you do," she said, sincerity pouring through.

He gave the familiar space a final glance. "See you, house," he murmured, his bittersweet smile and heavy voice full of memories. Turning to Abby, he winked playfully, adding a dash of warmth to their farewell. "See ya, kiddo." His words hung in the air as he left.

Travis passed by Talia as she entered the home, shouldering an expensive purse on one arm and holding papers in her hand. She smiled politely as they navigated one another in the foyer.

"Have you sold the house already, my love?" she asked Abby once Travis had gotten into his car.

"If only it were that easy," Abby laughed. "No, that was my brother-in-law, Travis. He came to say goodbye to the house. He lived here with my sister…when they were married," she explained, careful not to have to say directly that they lived here before Grace died.

"Oh," Talia sighed knowingly. "There's already quite a bit of buzz about the house. I think we'll be busy today, and we were lucky with the weather. It's a warm and sunny Spring day."

"Not as warm as where I'll be this time tomorrow," Abby joked.

"You're really doing it? I think that's fantastic," Talia said.

"Me too. It's something I need to get out of my system. A month in another country ought to clear my head. I need some time away from here to process everything."

“Have you given any more thought as to where you’ll live when you get back?”

“I’m trying not to plan too far ahead. I might rent for a couple of months until I settle down somewhere.” Abby knew what Talia was getting at.

“Well, I’m only a phone call or a message away if you need me to have a place arranged for you,” Talia said. “Morgan and I have become good friends over the last few weeks.”

Abby smiled, fuelled by happiness at the thought of Talia’s budding friendship with her assistant. “Good. He’s helped me so much with all of the changes I’m making in the business…and in my life. I’m glad he’s been easy for you to work with.”

“Let’s not get carried away. I never said he was easy to work with,” she said with a small chuckle. “But he is wonderful and fabulous, and that absolutely makes up for it.”

The two women’s laughter rose like a joyful melody, brightening the room.

“I know I put you in an awkward position,” Abby said sombrely after a moment’s pause. “I really didn’t trust this in anyone else’s hands but yours.”

“Don’t be silly. I was desperate for something to get my hands on. I haven’t been working much since Derek passed away, and this was just the thing to bring a little light back into my life.”

“You were such an amazing comfort to me after my parents’ accident,” Abby recalled. “I remember the day you arrived at the house. Checking in on all of us with your casseroles like we were the Party of Three gang.”

“I’ve always felt…connected to you,” Talia said. “I can’t explain it.”

"I feel it too. I always assumed it had something to do with Josh." She admitted shyly.

"I think you might be right," Talia said curiously, though not wanting to pry.

"How is he?" Abby finally asked.

"He's about as good as you can imagine. He's busy with work," Talia revealed. "That's as much as he'll share with his mother, anyhow."

"I shouldn't be asking anyway, I'm sorry."

"I do hope you two eventually find your way back to each other," Talia said gently. "I've always been rooting for the two of you."

"Thanks, Talia," Abby said. "I can't thank you enough for everything you've done for me. You're like my guardian angel."

Talia touched Abby's arm affectionately. "Everyone is someone's angel."

"Can you do me a favour? Can you just…can you let him know that nothing's changed? Tell him that for me, please. He'll know what it means."

"Of course," Talia agreed, "but darling, look around," she told her, looking proudly through the house before landing on a pile of travel documents peeking out from Abby's purse. "Everything's changed."

Abby absorbed it all, her shoulder sagging as she turned Talia's words over in her mind.

"And maybe that's the key to all of it," Talia said. "You don't like the way that something's going? Change it."

Abby glanced up at Talia, a tight, but hopeful smile spreading through her lips. "I'm working on it."

"I see a woman putting herself first. And there's nothing more revolutionary than that. Your whole life is going to change for the better. You go enjoy the ride," Talia said, nodding at Abby's luggage in the living room. "Let me take care of the details here. I'll email you the paperwork to sign when we've got a solid offer."

"I should get going," Abby said suddenly, not wanting to drag out her imminent departure.

Talia nodded and moved in to hug her. "Enjoy the start of the rest of your life," she whispered into Abby's ear.

"Thank you," Abby mouthed back, her eyes glistening with unshed tears.

Standing at the threshold with her purse on her shoulder and a tight grip on her extended suitcase handle, Abby took a deep breath and whispered, "Goodbye, house." Gathering her courage, she added, "Bye, Mom and Dad," before quietly calling out, "Bye, Sis."

Chapter 44: A WAITING GAME

June 21st, 2026

He sat himself on the first empty bench he spotted after parking his truck near the shoreline. Determined to remain there, solidly fixed to that bench until he had an answer, or a sign, or anything that would indicate that the rest of his life could begin.

With or without her.

Desperately praying for it to be *with* her.

Unable to imagine a world *without*.

He wondered if he was too early, or too late. It was just after three. They always came down here in the afternoons. In the early days, it was right after he picked her up from school. Tonight, he'd wait at least until it got dark. They'd been down here sometimes at sunset, depending on the time of year. This time of year, sunset wasn't for another six hours.

He briefly questioned if he was in the right place. But of course he was. Where else on earth did they have as much history as they had at Point Pleasant Park? The route to downtown's South End looked vastly different from the way it had on those days over twenty years ago. Tall buildings filled with sleek modern condos had transformed the city's skyline at a rapid pace over the past decade. But the park—the view of the ebbing tide from the very bench he sat on—appeared the same as it had when they were young, and dumb, and unbearably in love.

He found himself transported back to that night when they ended up on a bench just like this one, a little further down the gravel path. They'd been reeling from forbidden kisses and a Thanksgiving gone awry. Grace had been theatrical and infuriating; he could look back fondly on her performance now, though, at the time, it was a devastating blow to a situation that was doomed from the moment he moved in with the orphaned Conrad sisters.

A week spent sitting in his truck with Abby in this park, saying little with their mouths, saying plenty with their aching restraint, had driven him crazy. He convinced her to get out of the truck and walk the path. To sit on the bench and let the cool salt air swirl between them as if it could act as a deterrent. All he'd been wanting to do for the entire week with her beside him in his truck was kiss her, but he held back because he knew she was scared of everything that would come afterward.

A subtle hint of vanilla drifted past him, merging with the ocean's scent as he recalled her. He grinned quietly at his own skill in conjuring her phantom aroma simply by remembering his longing for her.

"Are you early, or am I late?" she whispered, bending to his ear from behind him.

"Well, let's see," he said, turning a relieved face to greet her, "I've been waiting for you for twenty years, so the answer really depends on what you've got to say."

She suddenly felt very stupid for having asked him to wait for her in the first place. Sure, she'd needed the year to eat-pray-love herself back to some semblance of a healthy, well-rested woman, but she still couldn't quite understand how he could wait so patiently for her.

"You want me to cut to the chase, huh?" she teased. Laughing through her nerves. Shaking off the shock of seeing him again. In this park. With those eyes of his, dark and beautiful. His wavy black hair, unaffected by time. The exact degree of stubble that made him look permanently undone.

She wondered how long he'd been here. Had he been counting down the days as she had, giddy with excitement as their reunion drew near? Perhaps he was eager to rip the band-aid, to tell her that a year apart had given him the perspective he needed to say goodbye for good.

"It might save us a decade or two," he joked, glancing back out at the water.

"Josh," she said breathily, staring down at him after walking around the bench to face him.

"Oh no," he interrupted, "you don't get to *Josh* me in your seductive whisper voice without telling me your decision first."

"I wasn't aware that I had a seductive whisper voice," she objected.

"Yes, you were," he said, side-eyeing her as she walked past to take a seat beside him.

He maintained a stubborn eye on the horizon, like a ship's captain, convinced that a storm was hidden just out of sight.

She straightened her back and brushed the hair from her face. “Are you going to at least look at me when I tell you that I want us to start our life together?”

Josh spun his head quickly to face her, his mouth clumsily hanging open and turning into a smile as his expression caught up with his understanding.

“Today,” she asserted. “Right now,” she added before shyly posing, “if you’ll still have me.”

Overwhelmed by joy, Josh could no longer hide his reaction. At a loss for words, he just nodded, then finally blurted, “Bout time.”

Taking her hand in his, he rested their clasped fingers on top of his leg. They stared out at the water for a few seconds, their minds equally, blissfully content. Free from the apprehension that had once shadowed every touch, they finally felt aligned.

This time, it was for real.

Abby couldn’t put a pin on what distinguished this time from every other. Maybe it was age, or time, or the clarity that had evolved from putting herself first. There was no mistaking the permanence of her intention this time. And there was no way he’d accept anything other than forever.

“So what have you been up to for the last year?” she asked cheekily, breaking through their silent celebration.

He gathered a full inhale before saying, “Oh, a bit of this and a bit of that. Work, mostly.”

She nodded slowly. “Any projects of interest?”

“Do you remember when we were here one day back then, and I asked you how you saw us in the future?”

“Of course,” she answered. “I always thought it would be cool to live in one of those houses over there.” Abby gestured to the shoreline, across the mouth of the Northwest Arm.

"Do you remember what else you said you wanted?"

Curious about where his interrogation might lead, she gleefully recalled the details of her adolescent daydream. "A porch swing."

"I built you a porch swing, Abby," he told her, a childlike twinkle dancing in his eyes.

"Thank you," she said, her surprise turning her tone more formal. She continued somewhat reluctantly, "Josh, I don't have a porch. I don't even have a house. I sold the house. I thought your mother might have mentioned it to you."

"She did," he revealed. "I wasn't thinking of the Conrad house when I built it. I was thinking about that house over there," he said, pointing at a specific waterfront home in the same area she had just indicated.

"You built me a porch swing for that house over there," she chuckled. "Do you know the owner?"

"Yeah," he admitted, letting a shallow wave roll over the rocks on the shore and withdraw again before continuing. "You're looking at him." Josh's eyes raced to hers, holding her gaze like a sailor steering by the North Star. "If you'll still have me."

Abby gently cradled his face, her palms warm against his skin, pulling him closer. "Let me give you…some good memories," she whispered before their lips finally met.

A year's worth of uncertainty dissolved. The world around them slipped from focus, leaving only the peaceful ease of their reunion.

The tide rolled in, steady and sure, as if it had always known they would find their way back.

Chapter 45: A FINE WINE

May 14th, 2032

On a Friday night, indistinguishable from many others since the day their lives came together for good, they were lazily sprawled on the sofa. Photos of her family, and some of his, lined the mantle above the dying crackle of a small fire. Their loved ones' smiling faces flanked one picture of Josh and Abby together in the centre. The only one taken that day.

Her legs stretched out, resting on his lap. He absentmindedly rubbed his thumb into the arch of her foot while scrolling social media with his other hand. Warm lamp light filled the house, illuminating a path from their bedroom to the living room and further into the dim glow of the kitchen. The harbour whispered in the dusk, the familiar waters stirring just past their drive.

She could faintly hear the babble of chatter on the videos playing in his palm, his algorithm acutely tuned to woodworking clips, which, much to his disdain, would whittle countless hours of craftsmanship into a twenty-second reel.

"This is what we're competing with," he said. "Everyone's lost sight of how much time goes into this type of work."

"I know," she eagerly agreed, putting aside her book. "I had to tell a young client the same thing—to make her understand that Italian marble can't be sourced and shipped in a couple of days like it's coming from Amazon Prime."

"Are we those people now?" Josh asked jokingly. "Are we at the '*back in my day...*' phase of life?"

"I'm afraid so," she admitted, smiling with her eyes over the rim of her e-reader.

"Some things have gotten better with time, haven't they?" he asked, his hand beginning to wander up her calf, above her knee, then inching its way toward her thigh.

"You've aged like a fine wine, Joshua Stone," Abby uttered breathily while she set the Kindle aside. She placed her glasses on an ottoman near the sofa and glanced down at his hand grazing between her legs.

He shifted across the corner of the sectional to ease himself over her. "So, you're telling me you don't buy into this culture of instant gratification?" he purred, nuzzling into her neck.

She slowly ran her fingers through his greying hair. "Some things are worth the wait."

He paused his hungry pursuit of her, getting lost in the depth of her gaze, the very woman he'd spent so much of his life pursuing.

"Abigail Stone, I couldn't agree more," he said before his yearning lips fell softly onto hers.

Blissfully unaware of everything still yet to come.

Epilogue

A BOOKEND

July 26th, 2052 – Halifax, NS

Alex eased the car to a stop in front of the house, with the gloomy summer sky hanging over the once-thriving craftsman home. The electric buzz of power tools got louder as he walked toward a woodshop beside the garage. Josh powered down the mitre saw when he caught a glimpse of his stepson approaching.

"What are you building?" Alex asked, unsurprised to find Josh burying himself in a new project.

Josh slid his safety glasses up and off his head; his hair more salt than pepper now. He adjusted his back, easing into an upright posture, his bones more sore than not. He wore a faint smile in place of a greeting. "I figure Debbie could use a few more pieces for her new place. That stuff from Ikea doesn't last."

"She's nineteen, Josh. She and her roommates are supposed to have crappy furniture in their first college apartment."

"Nonsense," he objected. "Anyway, it's just a bookshelf and a few tables."

"Made by an award-winning carpenter," Alex pointed out.

"Where's Janey?" Josh glanced behind Alex to see if she had driven with him.

"She's with Debbie at the warehouse still. They should be here in a bit," Alex told him.

"The more furniture they want to keep, the less we have to move," Josh stated.

"It's nice of you to let them have their pick of Mom's stuff," Alex said.

Josh moved slowly around the saw table. He wiped his hands on his jeans, then wiped his brow with the back of his hand. He'd gotten harder in the last year. More curt with his words as he became less willing to part with them. "It seemed silly to keep the lease going on that warehouse."

"There are a lot of great pieces in there," Alex said. "Debbie would take more of it if she could. Jane, too, probably."

"Jane's studio apartment in Toronto doesn't hold much. She won't even get a place with a spare room for guests," Josh grunted.

"She's hardly ever there," Alex added. "And she gets to stay in some of the coolest places on earth for free. I don't blame her for keeping things minimalist at home."

Josh rolled his eyes at the mention of his daughter's job—Luxury Travel Curator. She called it being a realtor for vacations. She tested destinations, accommodations, and experiences for the super-wealthy. The fact that people paid her to travel before they did seemed absurd to him, but it was lucrative and left her well-connected.

He and Abby had drawn on her expertise more than once, touring Europe at impossibly low prices thanks to Jane's recommendations and industry ties. Hotels and rentals across the Mediterranean competed to host her for a chance to make her curated list, and years earlier, Andrea and Ben had bought a condo in Portugal with her help.

"Are you two still pretending that you're just friends?" Josh asked gruffly.

"You know I'm not much of a jet setter," Alex said.

"Is that the only thing standing in your way?" Josh responded, surprised. "You teach online classes. Surely, you can do that from anywhere."

"Sometimes I give in-person seminars," Alex said, clearing his throat. "And it's not the *only* thing. I was married to Debbie's mom for nine years."

"You've been divorced for longer than you were married, Alex. And your daughter is ready to start her own life."

"Maybe we'll figure it out one of these days," Alex said with a sigh, recalling all the times over the past year that Abby's sudden illness and death had brought him and Jane closer.

He remembered the night after the funeral, when Jane had climbed into bed beside him—not for sex that night, but to comfort him really, and to help him sleep without feeling like he'd been left behind.

"Where's all this coming from? I thought you summoned us here to get Mom's stuff sorted out."

Josh turned the lights off in his workshop and motioned for them to head back toward the driveway. After a few seconds of silence, as they were walking the short distance to the wooden screen door of the kitchen, he said, not looking at Alex, "I just want to make sure everyone's doing alright."

"Says the lonely widower," Alex muttered.

"I'm certain your mother still keeps an eye on me from time to time," Josh said, a hint of nostalgia lacing his words.

"You're probably right. I still feel her around sometimes too," Alex admitted. "I still go to call her every once in a while before I catch myself. I expect messages from her. I can't believe it's been a year."

Josh selected a beer on the fridge door touchscreen and waited while the mechanical arm fetched his drink. He retrieved it from the slot and held it up to Alex, voicelessly asking him if he'd like one as well. Alex nodded, and Josh repeated the process after handing over the first bottle.

"Yeah," Josh began after a large gulp, "I wish I could say that it's gone by fast, but every day without her is longer than the last. When we found out she didn't have much time left, those days felt like they flew by." He took another smaller sip. "And then she was gone."

The two men drank quietly together, each using the cold liquid to wash down the ache of their grief.

Alex sighed before he spoke again. "I'm glad we've got a few minutes before the girls arrive, Josh. There's something I want to run by you."

"As a matter of fact, there's something I want to run by you, too," Josh confessed. "But you can go first."

"Well, Debbie's been living with me while we get her ready to move into her apartment, and she's been pretty curious about Mom and about you. About my Aunt Grace and my grandparents as well. I've got a fairly limited perspective on everything that happened with Mom's side of the family."

"Mmm." A soft sound escaped Josh—contemplative, unreadable.

"But you were there for most of it."

"Yeah," Josh agreed hesitantly, "I was."

"John and Debra only had Grace and Mom, and Grace wasn't able to have children before she died. Now, I'm the only one left. Well, Debbie and I."

"I guess I never thought of it that way," Josh said, one eyebrow arched curiously.

"I hadn't really considered it either until Debbie pointed it out."

"So what is it you need from me?" Josh wondered aloud, cutting to the chase.

"I want your story, Josh. Yours and Mom's. And everyone else's by extension. I'm off for a few months, and I'm planning on writing a novel. I've had some ideas come and go. Then I realized that there's an amazing story right under my nose."

"What do you mean by *story*?" Josh shot back a skeptical glance, intrigue lighting up his eyes. "This isn't a story, it's my life."

"Think about it," Alex said, winding up his practiced pitch, "you and Mom had a love that not everyone gets to experience. It shouldn't…" he paused.

"Die with me?" Josh said, quick to fill in the blank.

"That's not quite what I meant," Alex said gently. "I just feel like you two should be celebrated. You fought hard for each other, and you had twenty-five great years of marriage. There's a real story in there, Josh. Something for Debbie to look back on. Something she can show her kids someday."

"I'm afraid we don't have a lot of time to get this story written down," Josh revealed.

"I was thinking I could stay here for the rest of the summer. We could set aside a few hours each day. I could interview you and have you fill in all the areas that I wouldn't know. Even if I don't get everything by the time class goes back in, I'm sure I'll have a decent outline by September."

"That's…what I'm trying to tell you," Josh said quietly, waiting a beat before he spoke again. "I'm sick." He took another drink to let the sting of his words taper.

The colour left Alex's face as shock set in. "You're sick…like Mom was sick?"

"Abby had brain cancer, I've got it in my pancreas," Josh explained. "I went my whole life never even knowing what a pancreas does. I wish I still didn't know."

"You've been to the doctor? What did they say?"

"They told me I could try this and that, and it might buy me a few more years. I don't want a few more years. The world's moving too fast for an old man like me anyway." Josh leaned back in his chair, his arm extended, holding onto his drink on the table, swiping his thumb over a bead of water. "I was never meant to be here without her," he said. "I just let her have a head start up there. She's got people she needs to catch up with. And we both know she'd want to decorate before I get there."

"Jesus, Josh. How long have you known?"

"There have been signs for a while—before your Mom died. I had let it go too long by the time I got around to getting it checked."

"What can I do? Does Jane know?"

"No, not yet. You can keep it that way until I'm ready to tell her, which I'm planning to do this weekend. I've already told Andrea, so she doesn't get caught off guard when Janey calls her."

"Are you afraid?" Alex asked him.

"No," Josh said firmly. Then he softened right away. "I get to see my girl again soon. I'm relieved."

"How can you be so sure?"

"What's the point of any of this if I'm not?" he asked, gesturing around them.

Alex watched Josh closely, storing every word, every cadence, like a collector of rare things. "Good point," he conceded.

"Listen, do me a favour," Josh said abruptly, sitting straight, prepared to deliver his instructions. "I'll help you with your story, but don't go diluting parts of it by issuing any of us some literary sainthood. None of us were perfect. None of us behaved perfectly. No one got away unscathed. But that's life. Sometimes life is clunky. I'm not sure how Abby would've felt about all of it being written down, having our lives become fodder for conversation among strangers. But I know she'd never say no to you, so make sure you get it right, kid."

Alex smiled, even as his eyes filled with tears. "That's why I've got you, to help me get it right."

"I've got to warn you, my perspective is a bit biased," Josh said.

Alex chuckled. "Isn't everyone's?"

Josh raised his nearly empty bottle up, pointing it toward the grown man he'd known since birth. A man whose name was an echo of his own. A man who was now determined to echo his love story with Abby throughout history.

Neither of them noticed the way the light landed on the wedding photo on the mantle a few feet away; Abby, smiling over at them, standing beside the man who'd loved her from the very beginning.

Their bottles clinked, and they finished the last of their drinks.

Josh nodded, seemingly pleased. "Good point."

The End

New Book Preview

The love story of Josh and Abby may be finished.

But every love story leaves an imprint.

My next book turns inward, examining the stories we tell, the characters we create, and the parts of ourselves we sometimes forget to question.

Enjoy this exclusive preview.

Prologue

CAN I TELL YOU A STORY?

Gazing absentmindedly beyond her reflection, Emma executed her get-ready routine with about as much alertness as one could summon on a rainy Monday morning. She reached for her concealer and applied a generous amount over the shadowed rings beneath her eyes.

Can I tell you a story? she heard him whisper.

What's it about? she answered curiously, padding her cheeks with blush.

"It's a love story," he stated, his voice low and steady. "A good one."

She glanced toward her bed. He was there, comfortably perched on the edge, like the room was familiar to him, though she was certain they'd never met before. His face was indiscernible, his features not yet filled in. Still, she could already feel the warmth in his eyes.

"What do you mean by *good*?" she asked.

"You know what I mean," he replied teasingly.

She was pleased to know that he had a flirtatiousness about him. He was probably funny too. Maybe even a quick-witted Scorpio like her.

She asked, "How does it end?"

"You don't really want me to spoil it up front, do you?"

"I need to know how things get resolved so I can figure out how everyone gets there," she insisted.

"One could say it's a happy ending, but that's all I can tell you right now. We'll work together to sort out the details."

Emma paused, make-up brush hovering mid-air. "How does it begin?"

"Tragically, I'm afraid. With a bit more tragedy sprinkled throughout."

"Hmm," she pondered aloud. "The last one was a bit tragic."

"I know," he said. "I ran into Kate. But it all worked out for her in the end, didn't it?"

"I suppose," she admitted. "David may not see it that way."

He leaned in a bit closer. "He'd be happy for her, I think."

She watched him now through the mirror as she pinned a few sections of hair in place. "How would you know?"

He shrugged casually. "We all talk to one another on occasion."

"Of course you do," she said, rolling her eyes.

"So what do you say?" He folded his arms loosely, eyes fixed on her as he waited. "Are you ready for this?"

She tidied her vanity, tucking everything back into a small drawer. Still speaking to his reflection, she asked, "What kind of a commitment are we talking about?"

He drew in a slow, deliberate breath. "A big one. We're going to need to cover a lot of ground. Remember, you said you always wanted to do something on this scale."

"I don't know if I'm ready for that," she admitted. "Shouldn't I work myself up to it? Maybe a few more smaller projects first?"

"I think it's too late to turn back," he told her. "I'm already here."

She spun around on the low stool, now facing him. "But I wasn't expecting you yet."

He tilted his head. "C'mon, you've practically been begging me to come forward." He lowered his voice to say, "You've been bored."

Emma sighed. "You're probably right."

"Of course I'm right," he said cheerily, as if it were settled. "It will be good for both of us."

"What else can you tell me about the story?" she asked.

"Hmm," he said in mock contemplation. "How much time have you got?"

"Not much right now," she said. "I've got to wake Rebecca and get her ready for school."

"Hey, your daughter's name is Rebecca? That's my girl's name."

"You have a daughter too?"

"I meant that Rebecca is the other half of my love story."

"No, she's not."

"Oh," he said, pulling back surprised. "Maybe you're right."

"My daughter's only five."

"Maybe it's just a coincidence that they have the same name," he said.

Emma shook her head lightly. "It's never a coincidence."

He slipped into an introspective posture, furrowing his brow.

"Her name is Abigail," Emma said decidedly. "Abby, for short. That was my backup name for Rebecca."

"Oh. Now that I think of it, you're right. Her name is Abby. I call her Abigail when I'm feeling particularly tortured by our impossible circumstances."

"Right," she said, rolling her eyes at his melodramatics. "What's your name then?"

He smiled. "You already knew my name was Josh."

She glanced away from him briefly. "That's true, I did."

"You always had a thing for Joshua Jackson," he reminded her.

"Well, I couldn't very well call you Pacey," she said.

He laughed. "God no, I'd hate that."

"You remind me of him," Emma said, nearly whispering.

"Of who? Joshua Jackson?"

"No." She met his eyes finally. They were a deep, warm brown. Darker than she expected. "Of Pacey Witter."

Josh arched a brow. "He's a fictional character from a TV show, Emma."

Emma felt the quiet thrill of something taking shape.

It wasn't him that unsettled her. It was how quickly she'd filled in his missing parts.

She let her gaze travel over him, slow and knowing.

His mouth curled into a slow, lopsided grin. "Good point," he murmured.

Acknowledgments

To those of you who stayed with Josh and Abby all the way to the end—thank you. Truly. Following a story across three books is a commitment, and I don't take that lightly.

These characters didn't arrive all at once, and they didn't reveal themselves easily. They unfolded slowly, sometimes stubbornly, over time. I'm grateful you were willing to sit with them, and with me, while their story found its shape.

If you began this journey in Book One and chose to stay until now, I'm especially grateful. There's something meaningful about seeing a story through to its final page, and it means a great deal to me that you did.

To my husband, thank you for your steadiness and support through the long hours of writing and revising. To my children, thank you for filling my days with perspective and reminding me what really matters.

And to everyone who reached out, left a review, sent a message, or quietly turned the final page, thank you for being here.

About the Author

Courtney Spencer is a Canadian author of contemporary literary romance that explores enduring love, emotional consequence, and the quiet forces that shape our lives. She lives in Nova Scotia with her husband and children, where coastal landscapes and family life often inspire the emotional depth of her stories.

www.ingramcontent.com/pod-product-compliance
Lightning Source LLC
LaVergne TN
LVHW091117080826
845145LV00008B/1954